An Administrative Handbook

*A View from the
Elementary Principal's Desk*

Larry J. Stevens

The Scarecrow Press, Inc.
A Scarecrow Education Book
Lanham, Maryland, and London
2001

SCARECROW PRESS, INC.
A Scarecrow Education Book

Published in the United States of America
by Scarecrow Press, Inc.
4720 Boston Way, Lanham, Maryland 20706
www.scarecroweducation.com

4 Pleydell Gardens, Folkestone
Kent CT20 2DN, England

British Library Cataloguing in Publication Information Available

Library of Congress Cataloging-in-Publication Data
Stevens, Larry J.
    An administrative handbook : a view from the elementary principal's desk /
    Larry J. Stevens.
        p. cm. — (Scarecrow education book)
    ISBN 0-8108-4021-9 (pbk. : alk. paper)
    1. Elementary school principals—United States—Handbooks, manuals, etc. I. Title.
II. Series.
LB2831.92 .S72 2001
372.12'012—dc21   Library of Congress Control Number 2001018881

♾ ™The paper used in this publication meets the minimum requirements of
American National Standard for Information Sciences—Permanence of
Paper for Printed Library Material, ANSI/NISO Z39.48-1992.
Manufactured in the United States of America.

Contents

Acknowledgments   **vii**

Chapter 1   Introduction   **1**
The Principal's Role   1
Day-to-Day Operation in the Building   5
Problem Solving   8
Typical Areas That Require Problem Solving   11
Time Management   12

Chapter 2   Administrative Style   **19**
Building Manager vs. Principal as Instructional Leader   19
Management Style   22

Chapter 3   Personnel Supervision   **23**
Supervisor vs. Evaluator   23
Classroom Observations   26
Evaluation Conferences   27
The Summative Evaluation   27

Chapter 4   Selection and Supervision   **28**
Recruiting, Screening, and Interviewing   28
Supervision of Personnel   32
Site-Based and Staff Involvement   34
Self-Esteem   34

Chaper 5   Staff Development   **37**
Staff Adequacy   37
Staff Development   38
Inservice Plans   40
Sources of Inservice Programs   41
Implementing and Evaluating   41

Chapter 6   District Concerns   **43**
Curriculum and the Principal   43
Central Office Relations   44
The Budget Process   45
Priorities   48
School Boards and Their Agendas   48
Policies   49

Chapter 7   Safety in the Schools   **53**
Security   53
Critical Incident Plan   54
The School Building   55
Check with Police   55
Involve Teachers   55
Preliminary Steps in CIP Development   56
Using the CIP Manual   56
CIP Contents   56
Crisis Intervention Teams   57

Chapter 8   The Nuts and Bolts of Administration   **59**
Expectations for Substitute Teachers   59
Scheduling Special Classes   61
Class Size   63
Learning Styles   63
Flexibility of Groups   63
Lesson Plans   64
Conferences   68
Team Planning   68
Cafeteria   68
Staff Meetings   69

Chapter 9   Student-Related Issues   **71**
Retention   71
Student Records   71
Report Cards and Parent Conferences   72
Incentive Programs   73
Entry and Exit   73
Traffic Flow   74
Rules   74
Consistency of Rules   76
Field Trips   77
Weapons and Drugs   78
Facility Management and Climate   78

Chapter 10   The School Community   **82**
Public Relations   82
Dealing with the Media   82
PTA/PTO   83
Newsletters   83
Parent Handbook   84
Two-Way Communication Channels   84
Special Education   84
School Law   89
Legal Aspects in Relation to Public School Students   90
Informal and Formal Board Meetings to Consider Policy Violations   91
Negotiations and the Building Principal   92
Administering Contracts   93

Chapter 11   The Future   **94**
Schools and Community Values and Interests   94
Planning and Coping with Change   95
Long-Range Plans   95
Vision Statements   96
Leadership in the Future   98
Summary   100

About the Author   **101**

Acknowledgments

Thanks and recognition are given to the following individuals for reviewing and providing suggestions for this work: Dr. Maryann Anderson, Mr. Geoff Groves, Mr. Robert Pollifrone, Mrs. Mary Mahon, Mrs. Barbara Hudson. A special thank you to my wife, Patricia, for proofing the manuscript and for sacrificing countless hours of family time during the preparation of this work.

Additionally, I would like to thank the Millcreek Township School District for the experiences, challenges, and successes that formed the basis of this handbook. I am also grateful to the numerous teachers and support staff with which I have had the privilege of working during the past twenty-one years. They have continually demonstrated the highest qualities of professionalism and dedication.

So, you're the principal, what do you do?

There are ways to avoid becoming the above.

CHAPTER 1

INTRODUCTION

You must separate the principal from the position.

The principal's changing role adds to the stress level.

The news media are an important part of any school's success story.

Address a problem before it reaches a crisis;
it is always easier than dealing with a major issue later on.

Principals can have more control over their schedules
if they have better time management.

THE PRINCIPAL'S ROLE

Schools fulfill many roles. They were once responsible for the three Rs of reading, writing, and arithmetic, but now societal pressure on them has resulted in a long list of additional areas for which schools are responsible. Driver's education, drug programs, foreign language, AIDS education, technological modernization, and parenting skills are now integral parts of many school programs. While the role of the school has changed, so has the role of the principal. No longer is it possible for the school principal to sit in his or her office and wait for student referrals, or work solely with teachers to improve teaching skills. Now the principal of a building is bombarded by parents who are upset about the lack of school involvement in social issues, low test scores, unacceptable school bus stops, the music played at holiday concerts, and the school's perceived inability to correct emotional and behavioral problems that some children bring from home.

The school principal is the legal authority within the formal school structure and is responsible for providing an environment where competent teachers strive to meet each child's individual needs for a successful future. However, within the school, other individuals or groups of individuals can influence both the children and how well they are learning. As a result of negotiated working conditions, teacher's unions have gained power within schools. Negotiating involvement in curriculum writing, influencing development of rules and policies, and empowering teachers within their isolated classrooms now affect what children learn. Parents, either individually or as part of organized groups such as the Parent Teacher Association or Organizations, are gaining power in school affairs. They are involved in decisions about student activities, school boundaries, curriculum content, and, in many school districts, school board meetings. In some middle and high schools, students have become part of steering groups and in some cases, school boards, where they can affect school issues.

A growing group in many districts is the nonparent taxpayers, who are content to maintain the status quo in schools, and often unwilling to support increases in funding for technology, programs that address student pregnancy, increased teacher salaries, or additions to accommodate increasing student populations. As these nonparent groups, some of which include senior citizens, continue to grow in number, it becomes more and more difficult for the principal to maintain and improve school programs, enhance school climate, maintain high staff morale, and meet the expectations of local school boards. The desire to improve the quality of instruction while satisfying the goal of school taxes is a dichotomy that principals face each day.

Today's school principal must have energy, tact, common sense, administrative knowledge, and a willingness to spend extra time (evenings and weekends) developing personal skills to deal with students, staff, parents, and community. The principal can no longer work an eight-hour day and feel assured that the building is secure and his or her duties are completed. Evening parent meetings, committee meetings, administrative inservices, and school-related activities, including concerts, plays, ballgames, and socials, are not only part of the modern principal's workday, they are required components. Unfortunately, today's principal must accept more than his share of blame and less than his or her share of credit.

Principals must have entered the profession trained in all aspects of the educational process. Finance, law, curriculum, student discipline, personnel relations, public relations, and special education regulations are only part of the vast background required of principals. In addition, skill in decision making, task commitment, goal setting, prioritizing, time management, dealing with difficult people, communication, curriculum monitoring, and supervising and evaluating are key issues in school administration.

Today's principals must attempt to separate the principal from the position. The principal is the person—the individual—who works in the principalship. The position is the job, the profession, the authority figure who ensures that the school is run successfully. The principal is the person who goes home each night, relaxes with his of her family, and has a life outside school. Too much attention to either role can hamper success on the job. The individual who spends excessive time on school activities, to the detriment of family, will face stress, frustration, and possible failure. The individual who is not willing to give up some aspect of a normal life, including weekends and carefree nights at home, and is unwilling to work beyond the eight-hour day, may be viewed as unprofessional, uncommitted, and uncaring. The principal must seek a balance that allows for a commitment to district responsibilities and a healthy personal life. This friction can cause additional stress and frustration for many principals.

The principal should be a role model to several groups. To students, the principal must be the symbol of authority, the person who has the final word within the school: who is not to be feared, but respected; not to be hated, but recognized as a caring, concerned person who provides a safe school environment. To the staff, the principal is the legal supervisor of school employees. He or she mentors when problems arise, acts as an intermediary when parents are upset, represents staff at district meetings, and evaluates teaching skills. To the parents, the principal is the person to meet with when things are unclear, school policy is questioned, or individual problems arise. To the local school board, the principal is the person legally responsible for the success of his or her school. To the Central Office, the principal is the educational leader of the building who is authorized to operate the school. To the parent, the principal *is* the school, the principal *is* the district, the principal *is* the district's educational program. Of course, the principal is only part of the entire system, but, to the parent who enters the school office, upset about a child's lack of success in the educational system, the principal is the educational system. The community observes the principal and forms opinions about him or her. Any school activities are critically evaluated by the public and reflect positively or negatively on the principal, the school, and the district. It is no easy task to be under scrutiny whenever in public, but that is the life of the school principal.

The principal is the legal, moral, and ethical representative of the school in which he or she works. In the public eye, the principal is the spokesperson for the teachers, the children, the support staff, and the educational program. Whether at a PTA meeting, civic luncheon, committee meeting, or media interview, the principal embodied the school. Because of this, the principal must know all aspects of the school programs and processes thoroughly. Knowledge of the curriculum, staff, extracurricular activities, discipline policies, and all other components of school administration is essential to be a successful representative of the school.

To the staff, the principal represents the resource for meeting all the staff's expectations. Special education teachers seek additional supplies, math teachers need more manipulatives, reading teachers want to attend a conference on new teaching techniques, and kindergarten teachers want new chairs for their classes. Because each staff member has a justifiable reason for his or her request, and the principal must decide how to best allocate funds. Throughout the year, and particularly at budget time, inventory, allocating funds, and ordering supplies and equipment are ultimately the principal's responsibility.

As the primary person responsible for setting the school's goals, the principal must oversee the needs of individual teachers, departments, and, in cooperation with district staff, new curriculum materials. These budget goals, along with general school and individual goals, form the framework for the school year. Principals need to review, analyze, and set goals for school improvements and new initiatives to increase student achievement, and must look continually for better ways to educate children. To be successful, principals should involve teachers in forming school goals and allow teachers to take an active part in all aspects related to goal achievement.

As goals are set, the principal must analyze each one to see if it meets anticipated needs. He or she must examine the roadblocks that might occur and take steps to overcome any problems. One process, as shown in figure 1 on the next page, used to plan for goal accomplishment includes the goal, subgoals, possible roadblocks, and timelines.

GOAL PLANNING

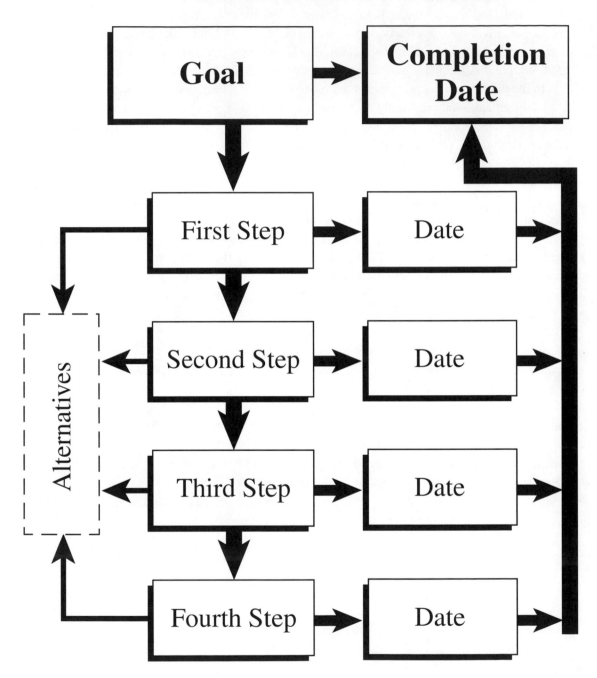

DAY-TO-DAY OPERATION IN THE BUILDING

Although the administrator's day may be perceived by some to be as fairly routine, it is often filled with the unexpected, the unplanned, and concerns initiated by staff members, hundreds of students, and numerous parents. Most agree that the administrator's primary responsibility is to provide a safe, secure environment in which learning can take place. Beginning early in the morning, the building principal confronts a world filled with staff concerns ranging from personal problems and curriculum issues to student discipline and recognition. Additionally, parent and community inquiries about school policy, requests for building use, and questions related to school programs often arise. As the leader of the building, the principal is the key individual responsible for all aspects of the building and staff. The principal must change his or her approach continaully, depending on the situation. One moment a teacher is upset about a particular student who isn't doing the homework, then a parent calls to discuss the grading policy, while the superintendent is calling about the next school board report, and students are waiting to be disciplined for fighting at lunch. Each incident calls for a fresh approach, a change in mood, or a different response. The varied activities of the school day demand that a principal continually shift from supervisor to counselor and from disciplinarian to child advocate. These multiple changes in the principal's role add to the stress level.

The typical routine of an elementary school principal might be:

7:30–8:15: Arrive at school and plan the day's activities: plan classroom observations for the day, phone calls to be made, and list of teachers to be seen.

8:15–9:00: Meet with individual staff member. Be visible and willing to meet with incoming staff members to answer their individual concerns. Be in the hallways to meet children and welcome them to school.

9:00–9:30: Make announcements. Check on custodial concerns in two classrooms. Read the school news of the day to the school population. Walk to two rooms to resolve problems pointed out by the custodian. Visually inspect the building for safety compliance while walking down the halls.

9:30–10:30: Observe a classroom lesson and record comments about it. Spend a full period in a classroom to observe a teacher's technique, then complete the observation form for a future conference with that teacher.

10:30–11:30: Meet with a parent on concerns about grading policy. Meet with another parent who had arranged a meeting to discuss her concern about the need for a percentile grade in academic subjects.

11:30–12:15: Monitor cafeteria. Move around the cafeteria to talk informally with children and monitor their behavior.

12:15–12:45: Eat lunch in the faculty room or with the children, depending on the day.

12:45–1:30: Discuss the morning's activities with the secretary, make a list of the calls that need to be returned, and plan upcoming activities based on the morning's events.

1:30–2:15: Meet with PTA president to plan next PTA meeting. The PTA president is concerned about the amount of homework assigned to one fourth-grade class. The principal listens, suggests a method to approach the subject with the teacher, and thanks the president for stopping by.

2:15–3:00: Plan for the upcoming report to school board. Based on the superintendent's request, begin working on research required for the school board report next Monday. Call to request documentation from another administrator.

3:00–3:30: Make announcements, monitor dismissal, meet with staff members. End the day by announcing the meetings to be held that evening, the inservice for staff after school, and the lunch menu for the next day.

3:30–4:30: Before the secretary leaves, review his or her work for the day and the work priorities for the following day. Return calls that have been recorded that day and log their impact on responsibilities.

4:30–5:00: Take time to review the day, assess the present day's activities, and list goals for the following day.

While this outline seems to indicate a fairly well-planned day, it is interrupted continually by student referrals, parent visits, staff concerns, and other unscheduled events. It is not uncommon for the principal to end the day dismayed at what he or she failed to accomplish. But, the principal should realize that he or she has had an impact on many individuals and an array of school-related issues.

Student discipline is an ongoing and critical part of the administrator's responsibilities. Today more than ever, the principal's maintaining control over student behavior can help prevent incidents from having serious consequences. One of the best approaches a principal can use in reducing student discipline problems is that of being highly visible throughout the school day. The presence of the principal in the building helps to avoid student discipline problems, reinforces teacher performance, helps create a controlled learning environment, and sets the tone for the building. Many principals make it a habit to be highly visible as the staff enters the building each morning, welcoming them and answering questions in an informal, relaxed manner. This approach to seeing teachers and other staff before the students arrive can reduce teacher stress, avoid interruptions later in the day, and help to create a healthy school climate.

Students need to know that the principal is in the building, so a wise principal greets the children every day. As the key authority figure, the principal contributes to students' feelings of safety, serves as a reminder of control and authority, and adds a feeling of friendliness. The principal is well advised to circulate during the school day, particularly during class changes, lunch periods, and at dismissal, to keep an eye on the operation of the building and to remind both staff and students of his presence.

In addition to being visible within the school building, the principal needs to establish a good rapport with staff, students, and parents. Open communication is critical if the mission of the school is to prevail. No one person, including the principal, can run an efficient, modern elementary school in isolation; it takes the cooperation of all stakeholders. This communication is enhanced if the principal has developed a positive relationship with everyone associated with the school. Staff members need to think that they can come to the administrator when problems arise. Students are more likely to observe school rules and regulations if they feel the principal is concerned about them as individuals, is fair and consistent in dealing with students, and is available and open to their questions. Principals need to remember that parents also must feel their school is a safe, caring place for their children. The personality of the principal, his or her openness and approachability, add to the feeling that the school is for the children, and that the administration sees parents as partners in the educational process.

The news media are an important part of any school's success story, primarily because they can help or hurt school initiatives and programs. Consequently, the principal should establish rapport with reporters and others. While the school is under attack or after a tragic incident is not the time to establish a good working relationship with the media. If media representatives are to present a balanced picture, they must be aware of school programs and procedures before emergencies occur. The media must know the person to contact in the school for information about day-to-day activities and breaking stories. Principals should be proactive in their relationships with radio, television, and print media representatives. However, in the case of delicate issues or matters of district importance, the principal should refer reporters to designated spokespersons. In most cases, newspeople are only doing their job. It is important to remember, however, that their job is to publish the facts and details of public interest. It is hoped that stories about school matters would receive balanced coverage, with both sides of the issue given equal time, but it is not the media's responsibility to protect the school system or to portray the school in an unrealistic light. It is the principal's responsibility to focus on positive issues.

Newsletters are an integral part of communication between the school and the community. Certainly, parents need to be aware of school programs, events, and happenings. But as stated earlier, a large part of any school community today consists of citizens who no longer have children in school. These taxpayers are becoming more and more concerned about the use of tax dollars for education, and school boards often reflect these concerns. Any effort made by building principals to communicate the need for new programs, the value of new technology, or the rationale for increased staffing can greatly benefit community understanding. These efforts can help to gain support for needed funding and pay increases.

Newsletters, often printed as Parent Teacher Association publications, allow the principal to advertise proactively the exciting things being done in the school. Among the topics of concern to the entire community are those that highlight students' work, emphasize staff achievements, list guest speakers, report test results, and announce upcoming events of community interest.

A sample article for the PTA newsletter might be:

FROM THE PRINCIPAL'S DESK

This year we are attempting to use peer mediation more than in the past. As we all know, conflicts are a normal part of life. However, children often try to settle their conflicts with pushing, name calling, and other violent actions. Through our peer mediation, we hope to help children learn how to resolve disputes and conflicts with the help of a third party.

The process will be facilitated by Mrs. Sullivan and Ms. Williams, and include the training of peer mediators to work with third-, fourth-, and fifth-grade students. It is our hope that this approach to nonviolent conflict resolution will:

- improve communication and problem solving skills;
- increase student responsibility;

- improve an already peaceful school climate;
- increase self-esteem; and
- develop an appreciation of diversity.

This building-based approach to providing a safer school needs parent support. If your child is having a problem with another student, remind him or her to use peer mediation. Forms requesting the process to use are available at several places in the building. Students should pick up a form, fill it out, and see that it gets to one of the teachers. However, both parties must want to be involved in the process for it to work successfully.

If you would like additional information regarding the peer mediation process, please notify my office.

The Parent Teacher Association (PTA) or Parent Teacher Organization (PTO) can be a great asset to the principal. Volunteers that serve in such organizations are tremendous sounding boards for proposed programs. They are the principal's eyes and ears in the community, and they can relay concerns of senior citizens, new families, and others who may be beyond the principal's range. In addition, they are in and out of the school all day, which allows them to form opinions about the school and its staff. These opinions may or may not be true, but regardless, they form the attitudes that are reflected in community acceptance of school programs.

PROBLEM SOLVING

Problems are a normal part of any administrative position. However, in today's educational world, the principal must prevent problems in addition to solving them. In schools, the principal must develop a means to find out about and analyze problems that arise, determine the best decision to resolve the situation, and bring it to a successful conclusion. An approach built on good rapport and open communication can help a principal to discover problems before they become critical. Addressing a problem before it reaches a crisis is always easier than dealing with a major issue later. Few problems go away by themselves; they usually grow in intensity and seriousness. The principal's visiblity and knowledge of the curriculum, building, and stakeholders can be a great asset.

When a problem is evident, the first step is to analyze the situation. The next step is important to gather all available background information. The principal must not wait until every possible thread of information is gathered, or it may be too late or the situation reaches the boiling point. Principals need to remember that, typically, any decision is better than no decision at all. Once the relevant information is gathered, the principal must propose various solutions to resolve the matter. Last, the principal must choose the "best" solution, based on the information available, the counsel of others, and the administrator's experience. Using quality tools during the decision-making process is often helpful. *Nominal group techniques*, *forced choice analysis* (explained below), and other approaches help to narrow and focus discussions. These participant approaches increase and enhance ownership of decisions reached.

Principals should consider using a problem-analysis process that includes answering the following questions:

1. What is the basic problem?
   Look closely at the challenge and discover the root of the problem.

2. What are the causes of the problem?
   List reasons why the problem exists.

3. What is the major cause of the problem?
   Reduce causes (forced choice analysis) to the most likely one.

4. What are possible solutions?
   List solutions to address the cause of the problem.

5. What is the best solution?
   Reduce the number of solutions (forced choice analysis) to the most likely one.

6. How will the solution be applied?
   Consider the various ways to apply the solution to the problem.

7. What possible roadblocks may be encountered?
   List and analyze the possible interferences in and objections to the solution.

8. What is the timeline to implement the solution?
   What is the process and how much time is estimated between each step?

9. How well did the solution solve the problem?
   Review and assess the success of the solution in solving the problem.

The principal must make some decisions unilaterally because of the time element or the fact that authoritative power is required. At other times, the principal may seek the majority opinion, consensus may be formed using quality tools, or brainstorming may involve staff in the decision-making process.

One particularly useful quality tool is the *nominal group technique*, diagrammed on the next page. In this approach, each participant receives a Post-it® Note and writes down suggested solutions to the problem, such as Causes of Poor School Climate. After each person has written several suggestions, each on a separate note, the suggestions are posted in random order. Then they are arranged in logical categories, and each grouping is given an appropriate title. The result is a large mixture of possible solutions to the question posed.

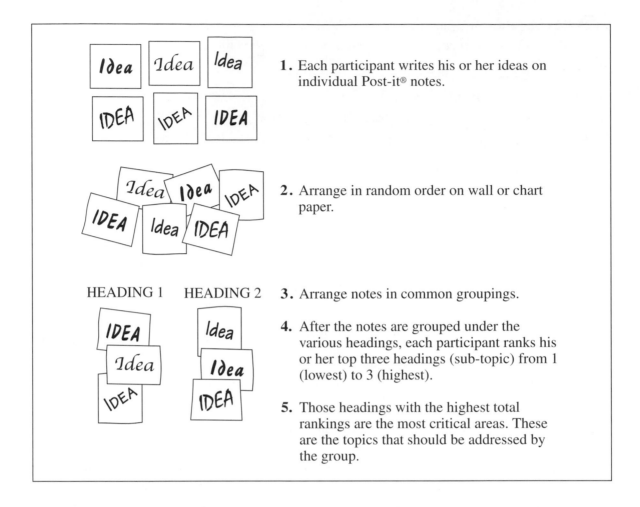

1. Each participant writes his or her ideas on individual Post-it® notes.

2. Arrange in random order on wall or chart paper.

3. Arrange notes in common groupings.

4. After the notes are grouped under the various headings, each participant ranks his or her top three headings (sub-topic) from 1 (lowest) to 3 (highest).

5. Those headings with the highest total rankings are the most critical areas. These are the topics that should be addressed by the group.

These groupings can be assigned to subcommittees, where further discussions can be held. This method is helpful in reducing a number of possibilities to a manageable few.

Another method to narrow choices in decision making is a *forced choice analysis*. In this approach, the problem is written at the top of the chart. All of the various options are listed down the left side and (in the same order) across the top of the chart. Then, the options are compared with one another, with a total of ten points assigned between the two options. The totals for each option indicate the preferred choice to follow.

Anytime a principal involves staff, those staff members feel a degree of ownership, and a successful solution is more likely. Principals must be aware of the residual effects of decisions and must exercise caution so that solving one problem does not create another problem later.

After a decision has been reached, the principal must act. Nothing is accomplished unless action is taken and problems are addressed. After the decision has been implemented, the principal must assess the results. Principals must be decision makers; the success of any school depends on wise decisions by the responsible person, generally the school principal.

Problems involving boundary changes, traffic flow around buildings, procedures used to supervise the cafeteria, the use of educational assistants, and other areas of school concern can be solved using these techniques.

TYPICAL AREAS THAT REQUIRE PROBLEM SOLVING

Transportation

Transportation of students to and from school, while a great convenience to parents, can become difficult for the principal to monitor. Students who arrive at school after being picked on and harassed on the school bus begin their day badly. Reports of student misbehavior must be reported, investigated, and corrected as soon as possible. It is difficult for the driver to oversee and control student misbehavior on school buses, but students must learn that their behavior on the bus is a school matter with corresponding consequences. Serious misbehavior on the school bus often results in referral to the office for disciplinary action. The number of driver warnings; a paper trail of past incidents; and a means for parent, driver, student, and administrator to meet and discuss the behavior and corrective action must be spelled out. A policy should outline various consequences for misbehavior on buses, including reassigning seats, removing the offender from transportation for a period of time, and mandatory use of seat belts. The goal of any school transportation system is the safety of all students. Any problems or incidents that interfere with the safe transportation of students must be addressed before an accident occurs. Ignoring such incidents can result in lawsuits, injury, or death. Principals need to remember that such problems do not go away by themselves; they only get worse.

Communication with Staff

The principal should hold regular staff meetings, in addition to maintaining open communication with staff during the school day and utilizing newsletters and memos. These meetings should include faculty meetings (only professional teaching staff) and staff meetings (professional and support staff). This approach enhances the "family" feeling in the building, as well as staff morale. Staff members (teachers and support staff) should feel free to suggest agenda items, and the published agenda should list the topic for open discussion and informational items that will be discussed only if questions arise. If no issues in need of discussion arise, cancel the meeting and distribute the information through memos. Regularly scheduled meetings serve as an opportunity for staff to share common concerns, discuss issues related to school programs and procedures, receive information about upcoming events, and air any number of issues related to the school. The agenda for these meetings might include the following categories:

- For-your-information items—Items which are not discussed, for staff information only
- Announcements—Key phrases to mention, which need little or no real discussion
- Time for speakers—Staff members who need time to discuss an issue with the entire staff (guidance counselor, department heads, etc.)
- A major issue for discussion—The topic of the meeting; all staff should feel free to contribute related ideas, suggestions, and opinions.
- Subjects might include the reaction to local charter school initiatives, creating an honor roll, better methods for assemblies, completing a survey for central office, and developing of a better parent visitor procedure.
- Conclusion—Reaching some kind of closure, making a decision, forming a subcommittee, or assigning specific individuals to complete further research.

Remember that each meeting should have a specific purpose or goal. Survey staff members periodically about the effectiveness of staff meetings. Such meetings serve to reaffirm the principal as the instructional leader of the school, but involving staff in meetings is crucial. Just as staff input is important in decisions that affect them, staff participation in meetings adds validity to discussions and ownership of decisions. Successful meetings must be timely, truly necessary, meaningful, and relevant, and should not be dominated by the principal.

TIME MANAGEMENT

One major element mentioned in educational reform literature is the principal as a proactive, educational leader. To meet this expectation, the building principal must be well organized and must use time prudently during the school day. Allocating time for the various aspects of leadership can be difficult. The prospect of operating an efficiently run organization where issues are covered in a timely manner, while allowing for the development of good rapport, positive school climate, active involvement of staff, and affective student behavior, is not easy to attain. This may be particularly stressful, even for the experienced, seasoned administrator.

Many time-saving techniques have been developed that have resulted in well-managed buildings, but they may have hampered interpersonal development, as discovered during research on effective schools. While creating the appearance of organized and efficient time use, these "survival" techniques have been perceived by others as too businesslike, impersonal, and uncaring, and have not led to positive interpersonal relationships.

To be successful as an educational leader, an administrator must balance productive use of his or her time with the flexibility to meet people-oriented concerns. Effectively run schools require logical, well-developed use of administrative time that permits the principal to meet priorities while fostering openness, sharing decision making, and empowering staff.

Issues to consider include:

- What time commitments comprise the administrator's day?
- What aspects of the school administrator's responsibilities are the most demanding?
- Can an effective school exist, as outlined in the *effective schools* literature, without someone to "manage" the building?
- What common behaviors and activities during the administrator's day would cause conflict with effective schools?
- How is the administrator's time divided among areas of responsibility?
- What techniques have administrators used to improve their use of time?
- How can an effective school result when the principal is so heavily involved in building management?
- How can productive use of time become a reality for the leader in an effective school?

Principals can have more control of their busy schedules with better time management. The secret to better time management is self-discipline, self-control, and respect for time. Principals need to consider their salary; calculate their daily, hourly, and by-the-minute wage; and then ask themselves: "Is that phone call, cup of coffee, or letter really worth three dollars or more?"

Perhaps it is. Or perhaps those valuable minutes could be used better elsewhere. Does the principal habitually handle matters he or she should not? How often does the principal spend time dwelling on past failures, regretting decisions, doing unimportant jobs, or procrastinating?

Principals should ask themselves the following questions to formulate a sense of time use.

1 = Never, 2 = Seldom, 3 = Sometimes, 4 = Often, 5 = Always

1.	I build on past successes.	1	2	3	4	5
2.	There is always enough time for the really important things.	1	2	3	4	5
3.	I make a "to do" list	1	2	3	4	5
4.	I try to work smarter, not harder.	1	2	3	4	5
5.	I delegate responsibility when I can.	1	2	3	4	5
6.	I am optimistic.	1	2	3	4	5
7.	I am punctual.	1	2	3	4	5
8.	I list tasks in priority order.	1	2	3	4	5
9.	My desk is neat and organized.	1	2	3	4	5
10.	I start meetings on time.	1	2	3	4	5
11.	I stick to business while on the phone.	1	2	3	4	5
12.	I use a time log occasionally.	1	2	3	4	5
13.	I set goals each day.	1	2	3	4	5
14.	I avoid procrastination.	1	2	3	4	5
15.	I make an early start each day.	1	2	3	4	5
16.	I say no when I need to.	1	2	3	4	5
17.	I schedule planning time each day.	1	2	3	4	5
18.	I reward myself for successes.	1	2	3	4	5
19.	I want to improve time management.	1	2	3	4	5
20.	I set weekly goals in priority order.	1	2	3	4	5

Where does the search for time wasters begin? First, the principal must look at how his or her time is being spent. Time logs can be difficult to fill in every ten or fifteen minutes for the busy educator. An alternative approach is to design a grid with normal duties listed along the top and ten- to twenty-minute intervals down the side. With this method, one only needs to place a check in the appropriate square.

It is useful to complete a time log such as the following to determine use of time.

SAMPLE TIME LOG

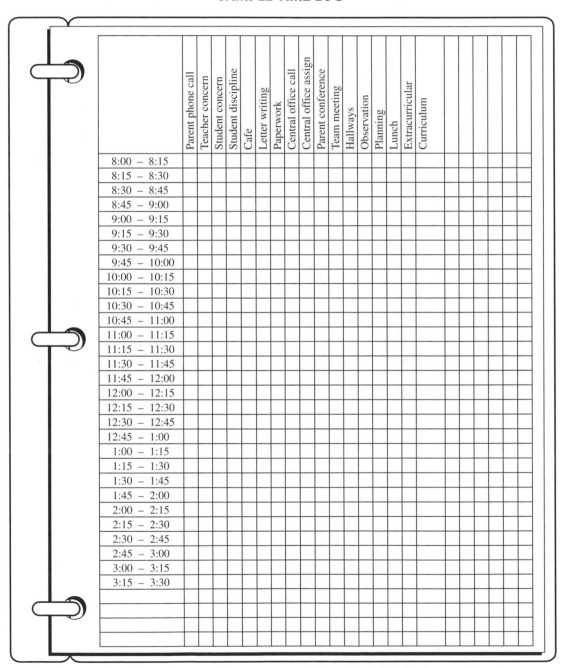

	Parent phone call	Teacher concern	Student concern	Student discipline	Cafe	Letter writing	Paperwork	Central office call	Central office assign	Parent conference	Team meeting	Hallways	Observation	Planning	Lunch	Extracurricular	Curriculum						
8:00 – 8:15																							
8:15 – 8:30																							
8:30 – 8:45																							
8:45 – 9:00																							
9:00 – 9:15																							
9:15 – 9:30																							
9:30 – 9:45																							
9:45 – 10:00																							
10:00 – 10:15																							
10:15 – 10:30																							
10:30 – 10:45																							
10:45 – 11:00																							
11:00 – 11:15																							
11:15 – 11:30																							
11:30 – 11:45																							
11:45 – 12:00																							
12:00 – 12:15																							
12:15 – 12:30																							
12:30 – 12:45																							
12:45 – 1:00																							
1:00 – 1:15																							
1:15 – 1:30																							
1:30 – 1:45																							
1:45 – 2:00																							
2:00 – 2:15																							
2:15 – 2:30																							
2:30 – 2:45																							
2:45 – 3:00																							
3:00 – 3:15																							
3:15 – 3:30																							

"Administrative Planning Guide," Edinboro, PA. L. J. Stevens Educational Publications, 1985.

Each school facility and administrator has unique characteristics that make most commercial plan books inappropriate. School leaders should develop and use a design that fits their individual style and circumstances. Spaces for student conferences, phone calls, daily goals in priority order, scheduled meetings, and observations probably need to be included. (Figure 4 illustrates one approach.) The important thing is to use a plan book throughout the day and keep it as a record of completed tasks, so it can serve as a guide for future planning and as a reference for accountability.

Principals sometimes are surprised to find that they spend excessive amounts of time on the telephone or sorting papers. Regardless of the method, principals should use a quick and easy log to record how they use their time.

Are mornings used effectively? Some school principals have found that thirty minutes of uninterrupted work before anyone arrives equals two hours during the busy school day. Some periods of time are worth more than others.

How many hours have been wasted waiting for meeting, a conference, or phone call? Could these valuable minutes have been used to plan, review a schedule, read an article, or jot down thoughts on the PTA agenda? Every schedule must allow for catch-up time each day for those unfinished projects. Only by examining of time use can one begin to get more important things done, do an even better job, finish sooner, and, ultimately, make wiser decisions.

Planning for better time management is crucial. Principals should obtain all available information, analyze it, break it down into its parts, establish priorities, plan a sequence and timeline, and then take action. Planning helps to set goals, and a clear view of goals clarifies approaches and objectives. After planning only what can be accomplished, principals should begin by doing first things first. They should pace themselves and schedule blocks of time to concentrate efforts.

If Tuesday is a fairly slow day, principals can plan work that needs uninterrupted blocks of time for that day. They should not forget to include time to think and plan. Many hours of wasted effort can be avoided with a well-thought-out plan. Good plans help to defuse many of the crisis situations that arise from lack of planning.

Instructional improvement is crucial to a school's progress. But when can principals find time for classroom observations? Would a principal fail to find time to meet with the superintendent, an angry parent, or a PTA group? Classroom observations must be scheduled like any other commitment. Remember: events that are not planned for and scheduled often are never completed.

It is important to set goals each day before going home. Arriving the next morning to a planned day is motivating and provides a head start. It is generally wise to schedule the most difficult and highest-priority tasks for the time of day when enthusiasm is greatest. Are you a morning person, or does the afternoon find you full of energy? Principals should monitor their alertness for a few days, and then schedule to take advantage of personal peak times.

They should use a method should be utilized that visually displays daily and weekly goals and priorities planned and met, along with conferences scheduled and actually held.

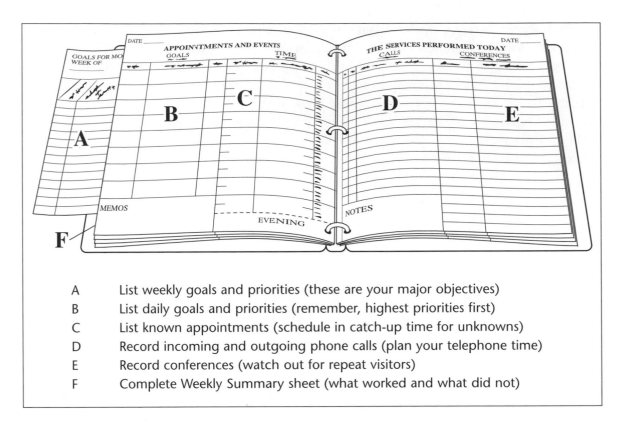

A   List weekly goals and priorities (these are your major objectives)
B   List daily goals and priorities (remember, highest priorities first)
C   List known appointments (schedule in catch-up time for unknowns)
D   Record incoming and outgoing phone calls (plan your telephone time)
E   Record conferences (watch out for repeat visitors)
F   Complete Weekly Summary sheet (what worked and what did not)

One of the most valuable items a school administrator can possess costs only pennies. Pencil and paper are one of the greatest time-saving devices available. The principal can record a phone number, a goal to consider, a message for someone, or a meeting date for later reference.

Pocket organizers are assets for busy executives. Desk calendars can also provide an overview of upcoming events whatever style is selected-whether a daily, weekly, or monthly-an administrator must buy it and use it; the savings in time will offset the modest cost.

Place reminders of goals and commitments where they can be seen easily. Placing a statement such as "Am I using my time wisely right now?" on a desk or bulletin board helps to reinforce objectives.

Some methods have been found to be helpful by others. Just because a task has always been done a certain way does not mean it cannot be improved. Administrators must look continually for methods of streamlining.

- Divide a bulletin board into three sections: Upcoming, Underway, and Completed. Place individual index cards with goals on them in the proper section.
- Use a tickler file with a collection of folders, one for each day of the month. As you receive a letter, memo, or assignment, place it in the appropriate folder with the date of the needed action. When that date arrives, the file reminds you to schedule what is needed.
- Microcomputers, electronic organizers, and administrative software have moved into the educational world recently. Personnel records, letters, etc., can be maintained for quick reference with these new educational tools. Time spent developing a working knowledge of the computer will be returned many times over.

- Use the telephone as a tool, not as a time waster. Think before dialing: "What is the purpose of this call?" Set a daily telephone time. If you are placed on hold, use the opportunity to complete written work or scan an article of interest.
- Arrange and make it known the time that is most convenient for you to receive calls. Remember, never take the time to write if a phone call will serve the same purpose; you will save time and money.
- It has been said that a cluttered desk is the sign of a busy person. In reality, a cluttered desk may be the sign of a disorganized person. Although a clean desk can become a fetish, it can also foster self-control and a desire to concentrate on one task at a time, which can make it desirable. Handling one issue at a time in an organized work area is a great step forward in time management.
- Distribute memos only to remind, clarify, or confirm, and only when they are needed. Save others time by having memos printed to read: "Unless I hear to the contrary_____." Or: "Thank you for _____." Design basic form letters to respond to routine questions. Use the bulletin board to organize individual reminders. Hold short, standing faculty meetings to announce items of information.
- Many hours are wasted doing things for others when a simple and courteous no could have avoided lost time. Do not accept obligations unless you truly want to fulfull them. Do not permit staff to hold you responsible for issues they should address themselves.

There are instances when planning time should not be interrupted, except for emergencies. A secretary must regulate visitors and gauge priorities. The organizational plan will suffer if principals permit everyone with something to say to wander into their office. If asked, "Are you busy?" principals should be honest and respond that they will be available in fifteen minutes, or they will stop by to see the visitor later in the day.

How many hours of work are desirable? Research shows that after eight hours efficiency declines. Set reasonable limitations and do not overextend the ability to function properly.

Delegate whenever possible. Do not allow such excuses as, "I can't trust anyone"; "'I'll do it faster"; or "I'm the only one who can do it right"; to cloud your judgment. Many routine tasks could be completed just as easily by an assistant, teacher, or secretary. Tell the person responsible what you want, monitor the person's progress, and evaluate the results.

Try to schedule meetings or conferences in blocks of time on the same day. Eliminate unneeded meetings. A statement such as, "I can meet with you for five minutes," is helpful. Whenever possible, go to a teacher's classroom for a meeting. It is less threatening to the teacher, and the principal then has the option of leaving when the business is completed.

We are often ready to work on a task only to find that the computer program is missing, the file key has been misplaced, or the paper clips have vanished. Save time by keeping supplies where they are needed. Those extra coins, labels, memo pads, and rubber bands will come in handy and decrease frustration.

Have a secretary sort mail into stacks labeled "action needed," "to be signed," and "to be filed." Use mechanical devices such as tape recorders, calculators, and telephone number files as organizational tools.

As stated earlier, an important part of a principal's position consists of thinking and planning; immediate action is not always best unless the overall goal has been considered first. When action has been taken and the result has been successful, a reward is needed: play a round of golf, go shopping or to a movie, or treat yourself to a special weekend. You deserve it.

A principal must train him or herself to leave their job at the office whenever possible. A relaxed home life, with a variety of interests, is necessary, and indeed is crucial to success on the job. Remember: We work to live; we do not live to work. The goal should be to work smarter, not harder.

Time cannot be bought, traded, or found in a hidden place. Each day it arrives ready for us to use as we will. Only desire and determination to manage time wisely are required. When time is scheduled successfully, satisfaction will be increased, and better control of your life will be a reality.

CHAPTER 2

ADMINISTRATIVE STYLE

Perceptions of instructional leadership vary widely among educators.

Every principal brings a unique personal approach to the position.

BUILDING MANAGER VS. PRINCIPAL AS INSTRUCTIONAL LEADER

Much has been written about the relationship between the terms *building manager* and *instructional leader*, and the role of the building principal. But the debate concerning these two terms is less clear when one considers a typical day in the life of a building principal. When the principal discovers a security breach that affects the safety of the children, is he or she acting as a building manager or an instructional leader? When the buses arrive late at school, and the principal develops a plan for all children to arrive at school on time, thus not missing any instruction, is that an example of instructional leadership or building management?

Few projects that a principal works on have no relationship to instruction. It is the rare principal who devotes all of his or her time to areas related solely to building management, such as safety inspections, food service, or transportation. Central office personnel, teaching staff, and parents make instructional demands on the principal that require instructional leadership.

Some have expressed concern about the emphasis on being an *instructional leader* as opposed to a *building manager* at the middle-management level. Many principals believe that most of the time they are building managers who also pay attention to instructional leadership, as some might define it. It appears that the major difference in expectations may be the definition of the term, *instructional leader*. There is seldom disagreement over the responsibilities of the *building manager,* but *instructional leader* may imply to some a more specialized individual who concentrates chiefly on implementing and reviewing curriculum. Some of the educational literature seems to define an *instructional leader* as someone vital to an effective school who systematically plans organizational and methodological improvement of the instructional process.

This author investigated the perceptions of instructional leadership held by principals, supervisors, and teaching staffs. Listed as valuable to instructional leadership were administrative concentration on being visible in the building, protecting instructional time, monitoring student progress, and promoting professional development. Not surprising, maintaining high visibility in the building, although desirable, was considered less important than spending additional informal time in the classroom observing students at work.

Protecting instructional time (fewer interruptions), monitoring student progress, and promoting professional development were more difficult for teachers to perceive accurately. At the same time, some areas, including pull-out programs, assemblies, and musical rehearsals during the school day, so often disliked by staff, are necessary interruptions of the academic day and often cannot be avoided.

Student progress is primarily the teacher's responsibility. While overall school test results are important, and the principal frequently is held accountable for them, monitoring and reporting student success daily is difficult for the principal to oversee.

Supervisors indicated that they needed better ways to supervise and evaluate instruction. The quality of classroom observations and the resulting suggestions for improving instruction were not reflected in the data collected, although they are often used by supervisors as indicators of instructional leadership. There seemed to be a need for supervisors to rethink some of the criteria used for principal evaluation, and thus perceptions of instructional leadership, namely classroom observations. Perhaps better assessments are needed that reflect successful teaching more accurately. Educators need to enlarge assessment instruments related to classroom observations and suggestions for improvement to include analysis of standardized test results, work in curriculum assessment, or implementation of instructional initiatives for improved instruction. In any event, if principals perceived more as managers want to increase their instructional leadership status, they may have to:

- change their leadership behavior,
- attempt to change others' perceptions of their leadership, and
- encourage changes in the criteria used to measure leadership.

Principals must recognize that supervisors, teachers, and they, themselves, perceive instructional leadership differently. There is often disagreement among supervisors, teachers, and principals when analyzing the roles that principals play in schools. Although some teachers may agreed with the principal's perception, principals need to be careful not to interpret the positive reinforcement of *some* teachers as representing the perceptions of *most* teachers.

While perceptions of the principal's instructional leadership differed among individuals, overall perceptions of instructional leadership were quite high in most schools. If the principal wants to alter others' perceptions of his or her instructional leadership, he or she may need to pay more attention to responsibilities identified more closely with the instructional arena. At the same time, to reduce frustration and eliminate feelings of disenchantment, principals should view their instructional leadership realistically. Honest self-appraisal and input from teachers and clearly defined expectations from supervisors can lead the way to better instructional leadership in the future.

Researchers should undertake more in-depth study of the instructional leadership duties a principal actually performs. Questions that should be investigated include: How are school goals communicated? What constitutes high visibility? What do teachers expect in supervision and evaluation? Topics such as these, once clarified, could add substantially to what is known about the principals' role in instructional leadership.

Areas of current interest to many principals include:

- What effect does the principal's instructional leadership have on teacher job satisfaction?
- What aspects of the principal's role are considered instructional leadership by teachers and supervisors?
- What methods, in addition to their self-perception, should principals use to analyze their actual instructional leadership more accurately?
- Do supervisors' and teachers' perceptions actually change if a principal attempts to become more of an instructional leader?

As mentioned above, evidence exists that perceptions of principals' instructional leadership vary among supervisors, teachers, and principals. Earlier research consistently found that principals rate themselves more highly as instructional leaders than teachers do. Teachers usually related the principal's value as an instructional leader next highest, and supervisors' ratings tended to be the lowest. But, there was consistency among supervisors regarding performance of principals in many districts, leading to the conclusion that central office staff were able to assess a principal's effectiveness well and to form common perceptions of individual instructional leadership.

It is interesting that the variables of staff size, number of classroom observations, and suggestions made to improve instruction did not correlate with perceptions of teachers. In fact, differing perceptions of instructional leadership were distributed systematically, depending on the role one holds within the district, because teachers, principals, and central office staff interpret instructional leadership differently.

Ultimately, whether a principal meets district expectations and supports teachers is affected by supervisors' and teachers' perceptions of instructional leadership. Instructional leadership may be determined by who does the perceiving.

The argument has been made that instructional leadership only takes place when the principal has a "direct" affect on the education of children; classroom observations, curriculum writing, and selecting textbooks fall under this definition. However, many principals feel that their role in today's schools is so interwoven with the instructional process that the term *instructional leader* includes all the aspects of building management. Principals see their role as synonymous with instructional leader and manager, both of which are critical to a successful school.

The responsibilities of keeping a modern, public school building operating effectively and efficiently are so time-consuming that many feel they leave little opportunity for meaningful leadership in curriculum and instruction. The responsibility of managers to solve day-to-day problems and cope with ever-changing expectations from a wide range of pressure groups, and still run the building well, leaves little time and energy for long-range instructional planning. Any principal who tries to rally groups toward a vision based on a creative approach to educational innovation often has too little time to do so. Such mission-oriented goals are better left to those in the central office, who are more aware of strategic planning and do not have to cope with the demands of building managerial responsibilities. Does this mean education (instructional) leadership is primarily a central office responsibility?

There is no doubt that observing classroom teaching, evaluating personnel, and paying attention to proper allotment of materials and supplies help to improve the instructional process. But, many argue that little real impact on improving teaching skills can come from two observations a year. How can improvement be expected based on visiting two classes out of several hundred in a year? Yet, real instructional leadership requires attention to setting educational goals through curriculum planning, helping teachers to develop their teaching skills, and providing both teachers and students with supportive services necessary for innovative implementation. Objectives such as these, although part of the *building managers* activities, are instructional leadership tasks. In addition to providing a well-run building with an environment conducive to learning, these tasks must be the principal's highest priority. An effective building manager is an instructional leader.

Certainly the modern principal must be able to conceptualize goals and expectations for his or her building staff. Unfortunately, the opportunity to make substantial impact as an instructional leader typically is limited to sitting on a curriculum review committee rather than investigating real educational reform.

The fact that contemplated change often becomes a hot political issue adds an additional roadblock to innovative leadership by principals. As long as politically active, yet conservative, school boards control district educational programs and practices, many districts will maintain the status quo. As a result, many principals will concentrate on a management approach to running their buildings at the expense of meaningful instructional leadership.

Such attempts to research and investigate educational change, with input from principals, appear to be more a role for the central office—but not because central office administrators have no more time than anyone else. Rather, policy direction is normally a strategic planning objective and implementation is a building administrative function.

Unlike many researchers and educational theorists, who prefer more isolated study, school administrators enjoy working with people. To such educational leaders, innovative ideas and creative approaches are paramount, and interpersonal relations are less important. By their very nature, principals, as products of the teaching ranks, are group-oriented and reluctant to seek isolation or work as independent researchers.

The modern building administrator must serve the dual role of building manager, responsible for maintaining facilities, and instructional leader, involved in supervision and improvement of instruction. When recognized and approached in a realistic manner, these combined roles can make for a balanced, productive school program.

MANAGEMENT STYLE

Each individual brings a personal approach to the position of principal. The role of the principal has changed many times. School management no longer can be dictatorial and top-down. The teacher empowerment union efforts and development of more humane site-based management have opened the principal's door to better group dynamics.

Principals are well advised to institute advisory committees, steering committees, or staff participatory groups to participate in decisions related to school governance. Facilitating such committees with a rotating chair, rather than the principal, helps to open lines of communication, shared ownership, and build increased trust within a staff. The days of the principal as all-knowing, all-powerful, unchallenged boss has been replaced by collegial approach and shared decision making. By utilizing courses in team planning and staff empowerment, and by improving school climate, one hopes that today's principal engages staff in decision making, improving instruction, and managing buildings in a more humanistic, less dogmatic manner.

CHAPTER 3

PERSONNEL SUPERVISION

Monitoring, supervising, and assessing staff is vital.

The alert principal must be aware of all areas of the instructional world.

Criticize in private, and praise in public.

SUPERVISOR VS. EVALUATOR

It is often difficult for some principals to facilitate staff one minute and then evaluate them the next minute. However, developing a good rapport with staff can ameliorate the apparent conflict between these two roles. Staff members who see their principal as caring, intent on helping them provide the best education possible, and concerned about the improvement in individual teaching skills, begin to view the principal as a co-worker and team member. As long as a principal gives evaluations in positive and unbiased ways and presents them in a helpful, professional manner, staff will be able to judge their principal more fairly. Formative evaluations (classroom observations, portfolios, surveys, quarterly assessments, etc.) of the teachers may involve a wide range of approaches, technologies, and procedures. The following are examples of teacher assessment approaches.

Classroom Observation

This is the most common method to obtain data on teacher effectiveness. In this approach, the principal spends a class period personally observing a teacher's performance in the classroom. Often he or she uses some type of checklist to record the teacher's behavior. Recently, more explicit data-gathering procedures have been used that provide more specific information, often in a narrative format.

Teacher Portfolios

To illustrate competency, the teacher prepares a packet that includes examples of student work, tests administered, lesson plans, notes on a unit of study, etc.

Self-Evaluation and Reflection

In this approach, teachers record their personal reflections on a lesson or unit. Teachers' reflections on their own teaching performance can be very rewarding because few changes occur unless the teacher internalizes the need for change.

Parent Survey

As stakeholders in public education, parents' expressions of reactions to homework assignments, communication with the teacher, and reception at teacher-parent conferences, etc., can provide a different perspective from that usually found within the school. Requiring a parent signature is often the subject of debate because some parents fear that a negative comment about a teacher could result in repercussions against their child.

Student Surveys

Student surveys often are seen as a useful measure of teachers' effectiveness. As the only individuals who witness the day-to-day performance of the teacher, students are well qualified to judge teaching abilities. Of course, students' age, maturity level, special needs, and possible retaliation must be taken into consideration in this approach.

Peer Review

Using fellow teachers as coaches, guides, or mentors provides the opportunity for teachers to seek assistance, feel less inhibited, and consult their peers for help. It also can be useful to have peers assist in judging the effectiveness of a teacher being considered for placement or tenure. Teacher's unions often object to this approach because it has the appearance of teachers fulfilling administrative functions.

Student Scores on Standardized Tests

Using standardized tests to measure teacher effectiveness is espoused increasingly by groups seeking better teacher accountability. Certainly, we measure the degree of skill in the industrial world by gauging the quality of products produced. In education the measure is more difficult because the raw material (the child) comes to school with a wide range of abilities and capabilities. Any attempt to use standardized tests to measure teacher skills requires attention to the maturity, ability, age, intellectual level, subject, special needs, etc., of the students in each class. Most feel that a pretest in the fall and a post-test in the spring is reasonable. In this way, the degree of improvement can be measured, regardless of the makeup of the class. Care must be taken that equity is used in such a technique, or the result may be few teachers who want to work with slow or at-risk students, who might score lower, and many who want to work with gifted or accelerated students.

Other Approaches

Videotaping, teacher research components, extensive staff development, advanced college courses, and other methods also can be used to evaluate teachers.

While a school district wrestles with the proper approach for teacher assessment, the principal is responsible for monitoring teacher performance. One component of this assessment is how the teacher performs in the classroom. Observing a teacher's lesson plan and technique is critical to good education. Some principals arrange a pre-observation conference before actually observing the lesson. This approach, sometimes called *clinical supervision*, allows the teacher and administrator to predetermine lesson objectives and set the tone for the observation. Others prefer simply to visit the teacher at a time the teacher selects. This allows the supervisor to see the teacher when the teacher is at his or her best. Still others prefer, or central office requires, that principals stop in unannounced to observe a teacher. While all of these approaches are acceptable, it is usually best for staff morale if teachers feel the principal is observing them to help them become more effective. When prinicpals are viewed as a threat, the mentor/mentee relationship that should exist between teacher and principal is at risk. Most teachers feel they should be treated as professionals and trusted to present a valuable lesson whether being observed or not. In the same vein, most experienced principals feel it is difficult for a poor teacher to fake a good lesson just because he or she is being observed.

Whatever the approach, a fair, unbiased assessment of the teaching ability of teachers is an important function of the principal. Lesson content, climate in the classroom, class control, preparation, summary, and students' success must be considered in evaluating a teacher's competence.

In relation to professional staff, instructional improvement is one of the major responsibilities of the principal. However, because teachers work in isolated classrooms, their teaching techniques must be observed to determine their strengths and weaknesses. As mentioned earlier, several methods may be used to accomplish this task. The quality of teacher reports, attendance, response to requests, and student test scores can be indicators of teaching skill, but nothing measures the true quality of instruction as clearly as classroom observation of a teacher's instructional approach.

This observation must be more than fulfilling a central office requirement. The principal must honestly feel that he or she is making a difference through comments, suggestions, and ideas about what the principal observes while in the classroom. In addition to supervising the professional teaching staff, the principal must observe all nonprofessional staff members. The custodian, secretary, educational assistants, food service workers, and other staff deserve a fair assessment of their work habits. Often this type of observation is less formal than those of professional staff, but no less important. For a school building to operate effectively, all components must perform at their best. The knowledge that the principal is aware of and continually monitors all aspects of employee performance serves as a reminder that everyone is expected to do his or her job.

Classroom observations often form the basis of mid-year and year-end evaluations. But all aspects of the teacher's performance should be considered. All staff should be fully aware of the expectations of the district and try to meet them.

Evaluations of teachers and all other staff should be conducted professionally and cordially. This is not a time to discuss unrelated events, but rather a time to spend one-on-one, between principal and employee to review past work and plan future goals. Discussions about attendance, response to administrative requests, working relationships with parents and other staff, and observed, documented job performance are appropriate. The outcome of any evaluation session should be an understanding of the employee's strengths, and areas where the employee might improve to meet district expectations.

For an example, the poor attendance of a staff member is often a sign of wavering commitment or other conditions that warrant the principal's attention. Staff members who display increased absenteeism should be monitored closely. Where there is persistent illness or excessive days out of school, these issues should be addressed by the principal in a caring, helpful manner. Often this change in an established attendance pattern is a symptom of family problems, a serious health problem, or a matter requiring administrative assistance.

CLASSROOM OBSERVATIONS

Classroom observation is one way to see what is happening in the instructional world of the classroom. Monitoring teachers' lesson plans and observing lesson introductions, content, motivation techniques, teaching skills, and summary remarks help principals to judge the effectiveness of individual teachers. In addition, test scores, response to parent concerns, and adherence to school rules are useful in assessing staff. Classroom observation should be a planned, concentrated effort to determine the teacher's success in transferring information to the children under his or her care. The alert principal should be aware of all areas related to instruction. A proper introduction, motivational techniques, and the importance of practice and hands-on activity all should play a part in the observation. The principal should highlight strengths and areas needing improvement for the teacher's educational growth.

Observation forms usually are standardized across the district. If they are not, or if a principal wants to devise an observation form, the following can serve as a guide.

The form's heading should display the teacher's name, date, grade taught, school, lesson content, and time of the principal's entry into and departure from the class. It also should include:

Lesson
    States purpose
    Achieves rapport
Motivation
    Arouses interest
Organization
    Lesson Plan
    Sequence
    Effective development
Method of Instruction
    Variety
    Effectiveness
    Provides for individual differences
Student Involvement
    Participation
    Group response
Review and Evaluation
    Lesson summarized
    Objectives accomplished

Introduction of Next Lesson
    Assignment
    Reference to next lesson
Atmosphere
    Bulletin board
    Projects
    Classroom appearance
Management
    Classroom organization
    Routine procedures
    Discipline
Teacher
    Knowledge of subject
    Personal enthusiasm
    Appearance
    Speech
    Attitude

There should be areas designed to indicate weaknesses or satisfactory performance, strengths or areas needing improvement, and whether the area is applicable. Some areas may not apply if, for example, the teacher is teaching in another's classroom, so the bulletin board is not his or her responsibility. It is wise to have space available for a narrative. Many principals feel that the narrative style is the best evaluation method because it permits a more detailed description of the teacher's performance. In addition to the principal's signature, there should be a space for the teacher to sign, indicating that he or she has had the opportunity to discuss the observation with the principal, along with the date of the postobservation conference.

Future observations should reflect improvement in areas shown as weak and issues discussed at the postobservation conference and agreed upon as needing attention.

EVALUATION CONFERENCES

When any formal observation is conducted or any negative behavior regarding a staff member is brought to the principal's attention, he or she should hold a conference, in private, with the employee. A good rule to follow is criticize in private and praise in public. Conferences should help staff members realize their value to the organization, the individual strengths they possess, and, if necessary, any weaknesses. For areas that need attention, the principal and the teacher should develop a plan to address improvements and establish a timeline for monitoring the requested adjustment.

THE SUMMATIVE EVALUATION

Formative evaluations, such as classroom observations, parent surveys, student surveys, etc., should be considered in reaching the summative evaluation. This end-of-the-year evaluation should serve as a summary of the teacher's performance for the year and include all of the summative evaluations. The principal should discuss all aspects of the teacher's performance, the result of such a summative assessment should be a clear understanding of strengths and any weaknesses and areas that need attention. It is a perfect time to formulate goals for the next school year, and recommend summer courses, or other remedial work.

CHAPTER 4

SELECTION AND SUPERVISION

*The basic reason for the interview is to match
the right person with the right job.*

*One of the most critical components of
supervision is the selecting and motivating of personnel.*

Ignoring poor behavior reinforces the behavior and says it is acceptable.

*For teachers to promote students' self-esteem,
they must possess good self-esteem themselves.*

Life is not a treasure hunt; life is a treasure.

RECRUITING, SCREENING, AND INTERVIEWING

Recruiting new personnel is critical to replace experienced staff who leave the teaching ranks. Applicants are selected through job fairs, observing student teachers, and other means. After a number of applications are on file, some method of screening the candidates to reach an acceptable number for interviewing is necessary. Usually you should select ten to twelve candidates to interview for a specific position. In addition, at least two different administrators should conduct this process in a fair, unbiased manner.

A team composed of administrators and, perhaps, teachers and parents should interview the selected candidates. A structured interview session with a consistent set of questions allows interviewers to compare answers among the applicants and select the successful candidate.

Principals interview to match the right person with the right position. During the applicant screening process, the principal should review each candidate's resume, application, testing results, and telephone/face-to-face interview to identify those people who are not appropriate for the position. Those not rejected become part of the interview pool.

After a group of candidates is selected for interviewing, the principal and team of interviewers must come up with a set of questions to determine the best candidate. Such questions might include:

- Autobiographical: Where have you taught previously?
- Forced Choice: Would you prefer learning support or emotional support?
- Rank Order: Please rank, in order of your preference, primary grade, intermediate grade, and junior high.
- Traditional: Can you share your feelings on retention?

- Closed-ended: Are you willing to work with students after school?
- Open-ended: How would you deal with a disruptive child?
- Probing: You mentioned adaptations; what did you mean by that?
- Reflection, then paraphrase: So, you feel that your experience qualifies you for this position?
- Self-Assessment: What words best describe you as an employee?
- Situational: If a student refuses to do his classwork, what will you do?
- Leading: Do you feel special education students should be mainstreamed into regular classes?
- Loaded: Would you expect a certain percentage of your class to receive lower grades following the typical bell curve?

Never ask such questions as, Are you married and does your husband work in the area? Do you plan to have children?

You can weight questions on the interview form or not, depending on the preference of the district. Occasionally, certain questions are more important than others, and their answers should be given more weight. Immediately after each interview, interviewers should record their comments and rate the candidate.

An example of a typical interview questionnaire follows.

ELEMENTARY TEACHER INTERVIEWS

Applicant: _____ Date: _____ Interviewer: _____

1. Begin by giving us some background information.
   A. College attended
   B. Certification
   C. G.P.A.
   D. Student teaching

   Other teaching experience (volunteer work, for example)

2. Give us 5 words or phrases that best describe you.
   1.
   2.
   3.
   4.
   5.

3. Discuss your experience with computers.

4. Discuss the steps you would take in teaching a directed reading lesson. How would you teach a new story to a 3rd grade group of at-risk students?

5. Discuss your understanding of team teaching.

6. Discuss your knowledge of the programs for students at risk.

7. How would you work with identified handicapped children?
   (Watch for individual needs, motivation, parent contact, etc.)

8. Would you prefer   ☐ primary   ☐ intermediate   ☐ either

9. List the steps you would take to address a student who is uncooperative.
   (Watch for talk privately, attempt strategies, consult parents, consult principal.)

10. Why should we select you as the successful candidate?

    A. Summary comment (a few words or a sentence will do.):
    B. This candidate might be more successful in:
        ☐ Kindergarten   ☐ Grades 1, 2, 3   ☐ Grade 4 or 5   ☐ Any grade

    Overall score: 1   2   3   4   5   6   7   8   9   10   Score _____

Principals should keep in mind that
- they should focus on job requirements, and not the appearance or personality of the candidate;
- most interviewers usually reach decisions within the first few minutes;
- interviewers remember unfavorable answers more than positive ones;
- once an interviewer likes a candidate, that interviewer tends to hear information that supports his or her impression;
- nonverbal responses also influence perceptions; and
- sometimes all of the applicants are overqualified or underqualified, and *no one* is best for the position.

The interviewing process normally follows a routine. The principal should do the following.

1. Establish rapport
   a. stand up and shake hands
   b. meet the candidate halfway
   c. smile and use eye contact
   d. offer refreshments
   e. provide a comfortable chair
   f. allow the applicant to warm up to the room
   g. keep it one-on-one (even within a team setting)

2. Ask questions
   a. vary the speed but be consistent in questions

3. Listen (for the meaning of the answer)
   a. don't jump in
   b. maintain eye contact
   c. anticipate answers
   d. concentrate on the responses
   e. allow *no* interruptions
   f. restate for clarity

4. Avoid roadblocks

5. Check references
   a. use references mainly to verify information
   b. when calling, don't say, "reference check"
   c. try to talk to the applicant's previous supervisor

6. Document the interview
   a. keep all notes and rating forms for at least one year
   b. if you keep even one letter, keep all letters

7. Don't compare applicant A with applicant B with applicant C. Compare all candidates with the specifications of the job.

8. Notify unsuccessful applicants
   a. say no more than is necessary
   b. thank them and wish them well; invite them to reapply
   c. it is *not* your job to train a person to interview better

In addition, interviewers should look for positive attitudes, clear answers, poise and appearance, and qualities required in the position being filled. Be sure to tell all unsuccessful candidates that the district appreciates their interest, and encourage them to apply again. Tell the successful candidate that he or she will be recommended for appointment.

SUPERVISION OF PERSONNEL

One of the most critical components of any successful school is motivating personnel. From the custodian who keeps the building safe and clean to the teacher in the classroom, from the food service worker who prepares healthy lunches to the secretary who greets visitors, all contribute to the school's highly structured organization. Each part of the organization fulfills an important role in the overall success of the school's educational program. As the supervisor of all personnel in the building, the principal must be aware of the work habits, stresses, motivational needs, and performance of each employee.

Employees move through various cycles during their working years. In the beginning, new staff members usually are enthusiastic, positive, and motivated. Then they settle into their job.

After several years a few employees fall into a rut. This is a dangerous time because employees who remain in this rut may begin to perform poorly, reject new techniques and initiatives, or change careers. This is the time for the principal to be proactive by encouraging the employee to attend conferences, head a committee, or take on more of a leadership role. This encouragement may increase the employee's involvement in school activities and help him or her regain lost enthusiasm.

As employees near the end of their career, care must be taken that these senior, seasoned professionals continue to remain active and involved in school life. Every individual has needs and wants to be unique. For some personnel, the weekly paycheck is enough. Others want a slap on the back for a job well done, recognition at a staff meeting, or a note or memo thanking them for a successful lesson. Regardless of the type of incentive each requires, the principal should understand that need and strive to fulfill it.

In any structured organization, some people are more cooperative than others. Even though staff have been screened, interviewed, and selected carefully, some of them may lose the drive and dedication they once had. These are the people who need the principal's attention as soon as the problem becomes evident. Conferences with the individual, help in developing new approaches and motivating strategies, and, if all else fails, warning letters may help to redirect the marginal employee. It is in the principal's best interest to keep an eye on his or her staff and look for any signs of discontent.

In the past, new staff members in a school setting were introduced to fellow staff members and then often left to sink or swim on their own. New induction programs have been introduced recently to help new employees to adjust to their new environment. Inservice meetings to explain district programs, mentorships with experienced staff, and time for additional training and help provide resources for entry-level employees.

Induction programs are intended to welcome new employees, instill in them a feeling of belonging, increase their understanding of their new position, and, most importantly, provide a strong foundation of support and encouragement as they enter their new position.

Induction programs should include:

- information on financial matters of interest to the employee;
- briefings on special programs;
- clarification of criteria used to assess performance; and
- a mentorship program that allows peer coaching, observation, and consultation.

Planned sessions should help and not burden the new employee. In addition, principals should be sensitive to the workload assigned and should avoid assigning difficult student groups to the new staff member with their discipline problems and numerous extra assignments that extend the workday and make it more difficult.

When induction programs that include mentorships and remedial help fail to address the problem, and particularly if a new staffer's poor performance is affecting students, the principal may have to dismiss the staff member. Few principals look forward to this duty. However, if it becomes necessary, the principal should go about it in a systematic and well-documented manner. When a staff member performs poorly, even while remedial steps are being taken, the principal must begin collecting the following.

- Review student test scores.
- Examine lesson plans for content, sequence, pace, etc.
- Analyze the employee's communication with parents.
- Be aware of the employees' relationships with fellow staff members.
- Systematically schedule classroom observations.
- Consider consulting other administrators, department heads, etc., for their observations.
- Make detailed written records of all conferences, including expectations outlined, weaknesses noted, and remedial action recommended.
- Communicate early with district personnel, including the personnel department and district solicitor.
- Pay close attention to any applicable contract language.
- Be fully aware of the employee's right to due process.

Principals must understand that a staff member who completes some aspects of his or her responsibilities successfully, but fails to meet other expectations cannot be ignored. To ignore poor behavior, such as tardiness, consistently late reports, and poor instructional techniques, reinforces the behavior, communicates to others that this type of behavior is acceptable, and, after a time, reduces staff morale. Fairly established and well-known policies carried out in a consistent manner assure staff that they work in a professional organization.

Most school districts operate under a negotiated teacher's contract. The principal must be completely familiar with and understand their contract. In addition to the binding nature of the contract, it answers questions that arise. The number of days permitted for death leave, number of assigned lesson preparations permitted per day, and remuneration for extracurriculum activities are examples of areas covered in most teacher's contracts. Principal's ignorance about staff contracts, whether custodial, secretarial, or professional staff, can result in grievances and reduced staff effectiveness.

SITE-BASED AND STAFF INVOLVEMENT

In site-based management, the principal shares many building site decisions with staff members. This approach to building management rests on the ability of principals to share authority and relinquish some administrative control openly and willingly. Caution must be taken that the staff, once involved, are truly part of the process. If the principal pays only lip service to staff input, this will have a negative impact on the process and cause distrust toward the principal. While staff may participate in decision making, principals must remember that the final responsibility for success or failure of school programs, initiatives, and budgetary processes rests on their shoulders. The advent of site-based management and the involvement of staff add an important element to the school community: ownership. Staff involved in developing and implementing programs, ordering supplies, and assisting in school management develop a sense of oneness with the school. No longer is it someone else's responsibility to make things happen. With site-based management, everyone becomes involved, does his or her part, and plays a role in school affairs.

Developing committees at the school level should be based on the strength of the staff. Many teachers have expertise, interests, and abilities that could serve the school well. Building committees composed of staff interested in reaching consensus, developing direction, and providing valuable input help unite a building.

Allowing staff to chose a committee (or two) to serve on divides the workload, builds morale, and reduces some work for principals. This type of delegation brings fresh ideas to the table, stimulates new ideas, and promotes teacher leadership. By serving on committees, informal school leaders can become more engaged in positive efforts.

Site-based management allows the principal to operate a school building in a manner that meets the needs of the staff and students.

While the goal of site-based management is total school involvement, some staff members may choose not to participate actively. This is to be expected. Perhaps with time and the realization that staff input actually causes change, most staff members eventually will become involved.

SELF-ESTEEM

Every person wants to feel important, and principals are no exception. But to develop a feeling of self-worth, people must keep in mind that what they do is ten times more important than what they say. To feel self-esteem, the principal must make others feel important, appreciated, and valued. The principal must highlight and remember their good work. It is always good not only to compliment an individual in person, but to tell others about that person's good qualities as well. It makes the praise even sweeter when someone hears it from a third party.

A principal cannot expect teachers to create environments where students' self-esteem grows if the teachers themselves do not recognize their own self-worth. Likewise, teachers cannot be expected to display positive self-esteem if the principal does not create a nourishing, enriching climate where staff develop strong self-awareness and good, positive feelings about themselves.

Teachers, working in isolation from much of the rest of the school, need to be reminded of their value to the organization. The principal should take steps to help staff members recognize their strengths and their importance to the school. Continually stress the vital part each staff member plays in the education of children. Mention staff's qualities at faculty meetings, praise their assets in individual letters, and congratulate them on their accomplishments whenever possible.

Being a building principal is a demanding, important job. As the educational leader of the school, you need to remember that children often react to the messages they receive. They are bombarded continually by feedback from parents and teachers, verbal and nonverbal, positive and negative. The children hear this feedback and it becomes part of their makeup.

Children with positive self-esteem have a higher tolerance for frustration. They can withstand more disappointment and the confusion that sometimes comes with learning. They have a longer attention span, are able to concentrate and remain more focused. Also, they display far fewer discipline problems, because they feel good about themselves. Name-calling and other harassment affect them less.

Those with poor self-esteem often express their frustration through misbehavior, acting out, and bullying others. They look to teachers and parents to serve as their role models. Students internalize the comments, actions, and remarks of these role models, which helps to form the students' view of the world. Remarks can wound and injure or they can enhance and build up a child's feeling of self-worth. They may have an effect on the child's future relationships and success in life.

As one of children's role models, principals should accent the positive. Try to phrase rules positively, stressing the good qualities in the school and praising what is going right, not what is going wrong. Research has shown that negative reinforcement does not change behavior. Children need to know that their teachers care about them as individuals, and the principal is the key person in setting the tone.

Help children to develop a vision for success. Assist them in setting reasonable limits and reinforce their successes with love. Principals must remember that the school may be the only source of love for some children. Keep in mind that strong, positive self-esteem is one of the greatest gifts you, as principal, can give children. Their lives will reflect the foundation they developed in elementary school, and the most visible sign of a winning human being is optimism-a feeling of positive self-expectation Whatever the task at hand, encourage the children to think positively, because they most likely will become what they think of most . . . success or failure. Self-motivation can help to create a valuable, successful life because expectations often determine our outcomes. If the children expect the best of themselves, they probably will achieve it by seeing problems as opportunities through focusing on where they want to go in life.

Children, and, for that matter, adults tend to work toward their current, dominant thoughts: thoughts of the summer vacation, the weekend at the beach, or the next football game do not lend themselves to academic success. Principals and teachers need to continually remind children to focus on what they are doing now. Yesterday is history and tomorrow is a promise that may or may not materialize.

Look for attitude as well as aptitude. The positive attitude of teachers and students can open many doors in their lives; it is not what happens that is important, but how they perceive it. If children realize their strengths, they will grow. If they see only their failures and shortcomings, they will feel defeated and frustrated. If they assume the traits of a winner, they will move toward that reality. If they visualize themselves as losers, they will demonstrate that to all around them. As Henry Ford said, "If you think you can or you think you can't, you are right." Lead them to feelings of "I can, I will, I shall, and I am a winner." When they internalize this feeling they will become what they do. Then excellence is no longer an act-it becomes a habit.

Build a school climate where children are taught to reach for the gold in all that they do. When you help them to demonstrate that they feel like winners, they are practicing those traits of most value to a successful life. They will begin to realize that no one can make them feel inferior, and that their best defense is always being at their best and choosing not to be a victim. Stress the value of enthusiasm and how easily it rubs off on others. Life is not a treasure hunt; it is a treasure to be valued one day at a time as they travel on their journey to a successful life.

What specific things can a principal do to improve a child's self-esteem?

- Be firm without being negative when imposing limits.
- Pay equal attention to children at all ability levels.
- Provide rewards for good behavior and consequences for bad.
- Express affection and praise often.
- Acknowledge good intentions, effort, and cooperation.
- Ask for the children's opinions, ideas, and feelings and listen.
- Involve the children in problem solving and decision making.
- Give choices whenever possible, and let the child be responsible for the outcome.
- Use children's names often.
- Help them develop a vision for success.

CHAPTER 5

STAFF DEVELOPMENT

If teachers are not intrinsically satisfied, little innovation will take place.

Principals should always budget for staff development.

Principals should use their building staff as inservice resources.

Change in teacher behavior is evidence of successful inservice training.

STAFF ADEQUACY

School boards are concerned, and rightfully so, about the number of staff hired. Given their preference, many principals would employ additional educational assistants, special education teachers, and support staff. When principals report use of staff to school boards, they should appraise that use fairly. Simply saying that a school has 607 students, and thirty-two teachers, resulting in a nineteen-to-one ratio, does not take into consideration the children's ages, special, part-time, and traveling teachers; and administrative personnel. A staff adequacy study weighs students and staff according to their impact on the school.

Before analyzing elementary school staff adequacy, it is important to define terms. In professional staff, *administrator* refers to the principal and assistant principals; *classroom teacher*, includes those staff members who teach regular education classes at least 50 percent of the time. Instructional specialists include guidance, art, health, library, music, physical education, psychologist, speech, and reading specialists; Title I; and other auxiliary professional staff not confined to one specific group of children.

A school's *staff adequacy ratio* shows the total number of professional staff per one thousand pupils (excluding special education children and teachers). In the calculatons, half-day kindergarten equals 0.5, and classroom teachers (as listed above) equal 1.36. Traveling teachers at the elementary level are given a percentage that reflects the time they are in the specific building. The principal lists all staff using the weighted percents below:

Sample school staff numbers:	
Staff in the building	Percent
Kindergarten = 2 teachers (0.5 × 2)	1.0
classroom teachers grades 1–5 (20 teachers × 1.32)	26.4
Support teachers:	
speech, art (.80), p.e. (.80),	1.60
music (.80), guidance (.50),	1.30

nurse, librarian, Title I (.20 ea)   60
principal, gifted (1.36 ea)   2.72   33.62 (weighted staff)

Grade		Enrollment	Staff	Value
Kindergarten	87	×	0.5	= 43.5
Grades 1–5	520	×	1.36	= 707.2
		weighted enrollment		= 750.7

Therefore, 750.7 (weighted enrollment) divided by 33.60 (weighted staff) equals the staff adequacy ratio 22.30. This is the *staff adequacy ratio* or the ratio of students to staff for the sample school.

Principals should know the ratio of staff to student enrollment, and he or she should notify the central office of staffing needs. While there are several approaches to analysis of ratios, it is often best to look at the number of students in homerooms as a quick estimate of class size. In middle schools where there is departmental instruction, it is best to look at each specific teaching station and the number of students assigned to it. Take care not to simply divide the number of students by the number of professionals in the building. This approach, which includes the nurse, speech teacher, principal, librarian, etc., underestimates the actual class size and student:teacher ratio.

STAFF DEVELOPMENT

Some feel that to be effective and satisfying, staff development should focus primarily on the needs of teachers rather than on those of the organization. The term *staff development* implies that it should affect teachers' knowledge and competence rather than modify the framework within which they work. Before teachers seriously attempt to implement an organizational goal, they must understand their own feelings and their role as teachers. Every organization should conduct inservice activities for new programs and curricular revisions, and such inservice should be district-wide for consistency. Remember, until teachers feel comfortable and instrinsically satisfied, little innovation will take place in the classroom.

Although school structure influences teacher satisfaction, other teacher-identified issues must be addressed in staff development.

It is best to try to relate teacher needs to organizational needs. Individuals are the products of their thoughts and environment, so the more teachers feel a sense of ownership and see a personal advantage in inservice offerings, the greater commitment they will make to the time and effort required. If staff development can help individual teachers gain more insight into their teaching and provide the catalyst for reexamining their approaches and techniques, then their needs will be addressed. The better that teachers feel about themselves, the better the odds that they will engage in critical thinking related to their teaching.

Teachers must feel personally safe and secure before they can overcome their inherent fear of experimentation. The more teachers begin to develop inquiring minds and find their own best ways of doing things, the more opportunity they will have for self-awareness and internal assessment. Staff development that is concerned with organizational goals will be seen as worthwhile only if the goals coincide with teachers' personal needs. Normally, once the classroom door closes, teachers seldom deviate from established teaching methods. While there are many established methods, teachers usually rely on procedures with which they are comfortable. If teachers' feelings and need for confidence and self-esteem are not acknowledged, little will change, and the status quo will remain in tomorrow's schools. The only way to ensure that teachers' needs are addressed in staff development is to include teachers in the planning process. The historic lack of identity with staff development programs has resulted in some teachers continuing to burn out, losing their enthusiasm for teaching, and perhaps leaving the profession. And if teachers leave the profession, organizational goals will not be met.

Staff development must consider the growth stages of teachers, before they can fully appreciate and accept the goals of the organization. Meeting the needs of teachers at this early stage is the necessary preliminary step needed before organizational goals can be addressed. Not meeting the personal and professional growth needs of these teachers at various developmental stages results in teachers disregarding inservice programs devoted to organizational needs. Within the safety of the classroom, teachers are free to pursue their personal goals, search for their identity, and attempt self-improvement of techniques, despite district-imposed staff development presentations related to the organization.

For staff development to have beneficial effects, teachers must feel that they are receiving practical assistance or usable techniques. Only then are they more likely to concentrate on carrying out organizational goals. Changes in teaching will happen only when teachers feel they are growing and developing as individuals, not solely in response to the needs of the organization. Without programs related to improved understanding of self, and clearer knowledge of the stages of individual growth, staff development cannot progress to include organizational goals. Only when teachers see staff development as personally worthwhile and satisfying can organizational needs become a priority for them.

Some districts approach inservice programs by offering a number of topics to meet a wide range of staff interests. A typical school district's inservice program is outlined as follows.

SAMPLE INSERVICE PROGRAM

General session and keynote speaker (motivational speaker)
  All attend in auditorium

One-hour required session (to discuss curriculum)
  Departmental meetings

Lunch

Select one afternoon session for personal growth

Tae Kwon Do and Self-Defense	Work/Family—Keeping the Balance
Understanding Alzheimer's Disease	Asset Management
Aroma Therapy for Stress Relief	Taking Control of Pain
Diabetes—Do You Have It?	WIL-LI-NETICS
Sexual Assault Awareness	Women's Health Care
Partnering for a Healthy Future	Disaster Preparedness

Lung Health
Healthy Eating and Exercise
Crisis Services
HIV/AIDS Awareness
Golf

Sports Entertainment
Retirement Planning
Massage Therapy
Wellness—Taking Control of Your Life
Heart Disease

Select one afternoon session to continue personal growth

Communication
Software
Video Broadcasting
Desktop Publishing
EasyGrade Pro
Using the Internet
Sky Watching via StarLab
Web Page Design

The Mac for Morons
Mail Merge in Appleworks
School Partnership Programs
Creating a Brochure
PowerPoint
Digital Video Editing
AV Technology for the Future
Computer Curriculum

Inservice Day conclusion
All hear final speaker and complete inservice evaluation

Principals should always be alert to the needs of staff members. Providing additional training and inservice to meet existing needs is one of the major ways a principal can have direct effect on a staff member's performance. Teachers who need to improve classroom management, motivational techniques, etc., can be asked to attend inservice programs in the areas identified as deficient.

Custodians can be trained in better cleaning techniques, and secretaries in new office procedures and computer programs. Principals should always include funding for staff development programs as part of the budget process.

INSERVICE PLANS

Staff development should provide opportunities for staff to acquire new skills and attitudes to improve student learning. Over the years, however, many teachers have become disenchanted with inservice offerings. Some feel that the time spent in inservice meetings could be better spent in other ways. They often reject being lectured to by some expert who is a stranger to their district. Efforts to involve staff in recommending inservice offerings usually result in more appropriate activities. Most staff members recognize areas where they need improvement, and seek training on specific topics that address concerns in the classroom. Committees of teachers and administrators working to develop inservice programs tend to meet the needs of most staff members. While administrators often perceive the need to improve the technological aspect of how teachers teach, including management techniques, and new processes and procedures, issues related to staff attitudes often are overlooked. In addition, for an inservice to be worthwhile, the presenter or facilitator must be a person who inspires trust.

Inservice programs for food workers, custodians, secretaries, and educational assistants should be directly related to their job performance. If you bring in an outside presenter, be sure the speaker is known by and previously heard by a member of the selection committee. Too often a presenter who was thought to be stimulating and motivating fails to measure up to his or her glowing press releases. If support staff don't see how this presentation is related directly to their jobs or the inservice will be a waste of time and money.

Principals should make every effort to coordinate inservice offerings with current programs. Principals should look to their building staff for ideas on inservice because site-based staff know more precisely what is needed to improve their school's learning opportunities.

SOURCES OF INSERVICE PROGRAMS

State departments of educations, school board associations, local intermediate units, book companies, etc., all serve as source of inservice programs. It is often less expensive to send individual employees away for training rather than to bring in presenters. However, staff members sent to conferences should share with their colleagues what they have learned and its application to district initiatives. When a number of staff members need inservice, or several school districts are combining efforts, using an outside presenter is usually appropriate. If staff members are aware of available funding, they often will bring inservice offerings to the attention of the building principal.

An often overlooked source of inservice presenters is staff members themselves. Ideas that have worked in their classes, courses they have completed, skills and knowledge they have acquired, are all fertile ground for sharing. An added advantage of this approach is that staff members trust and respect their own colleagues. Additionally, when new approaches are undertaken or problems arise and consultation is needed, having the presenter teaching down the hall is a great asset.

IMPLEMENTING AND EVALUATING

After each inservice program, participants usually complete evaluations similar to the one on the following page.

INSERVICE EVALUATION FORM

Please circle your response to the following statements.

(SA = Strongly Agree, A = Agree, D = Disagree, SD = Strongly Disagree)

1. The keynote speaker was insightful and interesting.

   SA   A   D   SD

   Comments: _____

2. Session 1 (department meetings) _____ was valuable.

   SA   A   D   SD

   Comments: _____

3. Session 2 (program name) was valuable.

   SA   A   D   SD

   Comments: _____

4. Session 3 (program name) was valuable.

   SA   A   D   SD

   Comments: _____

5. The concluding session was valuable.

   SA   A   D   SD

   Comments: _____

Please place your sheet in the basket as you exit. Thank you.

While this feedback may be useful only for future logistics, it does offer staff the opportunity to give their opinions of the inservice. Besides referring to the quality of the program and its relevance to staff members' performance, the evaluation should ask questions about future inservice offerings. It does not gauge the effectiveness of the inservice, however. Too much theory and nonpractical application usually result in poor inservice reviews. Experience has shown that because teachers often are reluctant to respond negatively, evaluation of inservice programs often yield little of value. The ultimate gauge of successful programs is improved techniques and programs in the classroom. Enhanced student learning is the ultimate gauge of successful programs.

Change in teacher behavior may be more indicative of successful presentations, but it is difficult to judge or evaluate. The principal who sees some staff members incorporating new ideas into the curriculum and making alterations in classroom instruction has evidence that the inservice was beneficial. Sometimes, reminding staff what it is like to be a student again-sitting on hard chairs, raising a hand to be called on, and practicing good listening skills-is a hidden benefit of inservice programs.

CHAPTER 6

DISTRICT CONCERNS

*The principal must set aside personal feelings and
investigate student allegations thoroughly and fairly.*

*Few things get a principal into trouble more quickly
than areas having to do with district money.*

*Lack of attention to small problems today may result in
expensive attention to worse problems tomorrow.*

School boards create policies, and the administration carries them out.

CURRICULUM AND THE PRINCIPAL

In some schools the principal may not be involved directly in curriculum work. In those districts where teachers and administrators are responsible for developing curriculum, they must take care to select a text or a resource that follows the curriculum, and not develop a curriculum that follows a text. Creating a local curriculum or a plan of study that reflects general areas related to standardized testing should reflect educational thinking within the school district, not a textbook company thousands of miles away.

Parents have certain expectations for their children and their children's school. When a parent objects to a book being read, a movie shown as part of the curriculum, or a teacher's comments during class, the principal must be responsive and fair in his or her investigation. Many school districts have a standing committee that reviews questionable books or films. This approach allows the principal to refer these concerns to an unbiased third party. These committees should include lay members of the community and educators. No matter what approach is used, the principal is responsible for getting back to the parent and, if necessary, making arrangements for the child to take alternative instruction in lieu of the book or film.

When a teacher's comments come under question, additional factors come into play. Often the teacher's union may be involved if the teacher's academic freedom is in question. The principal must obtain exact testimony from students about actual statements the teacher made. If remarks are found to be unacceptable, the prinicpal must devise appropriate consequences. Such consequences could include a mild verbal reprimand, a written reprimand in the employee's permanent file, or referral to the school board for dismissal. Regardless of the outcome, it is a very serious matter when a parent accuses a teacher of unprofessional behavior. The principal must set aside his or her personal feelings about the staff member and investigate thoroughly and fairly. Some districts have procedures calling for a central office team to investigate such allegations, which obviates the principal's involvement.

CENTRAL OFFICE RELATIONS

It is vital to establish and maintain good rapport with central office staff. These individuals not only serve as a monitor of building-level administrative activities, but also as reliable resources. One hopes they are highly focused experts in a position to answer questions that arise at the building level. Questions about curriculum, special education, finance, support services, and school board expectations should be addressed to the central office supervisors and directors responsible for each area. Their support and cooperation can help to create a smooth-running district and greatly enhance operation of the individual schools.

Curriculum often is seen as the keystone of the school system. It should include what is to be taught, along with the order and sequence of topics. The supervisor of this area is responsible for the overall coordination of all academic programs across all grade levels. In some districts this responsibility is divided between two individuals, one coordinating the elementary schools, and the other secondary. Regardless of the type of central office organization, this position is key to bringing innovative ideas into the district, providing guidelines for inservice, rewriting curriculum, and screening and selecting the textbooks and resources used in the schools.

Special education has grown over the past few years. The terms *inclusion*, *mainstreaming*, *right to a free and public education*, *individual educational plan*, *notice of recommended assignment*, and others have been added to the vocabulary of the typical principal. The principal must be aware of all aspects of the special education programs in his or her school and how heavily they rely on the central office supervisor assigned to the special education program. A principal making decisions regarding special education programs, placements, courses, or procedures without a thorough knowledge of school district rules and state and federal laws, or without consultation with central office supervisors, is not only foolish, but could result in his or her having a short administrative career. Most special education parents are aware of their rights and those of their children. The wise principal is equally well prepared and completely familiar with regulations related to all types of special education situations.

The superintendent and/or assistant superintendent normally coordinates and leads other central office supervisors and directors. While rapport is desirable and needed between the top leadership of the district and the building-level principal, most contacts principals make are with other line officers directly under the superintendent. Issues that might reach the assistant superintendent or superintendent level have to do with the legal aspects of an action, such as a grievance, information about a weapon discovered in a school building, requests from the school board regarding a specific building, or assignments made at the discretion of the superintendent. This office is the penultimate sounding board before issues reach the school board. The superintendent usually speaks for the school district and sets its academic and administrative direction. The person in this position is responsible for the overall successful operation of the district, staff, administrators, and, ultimately, the quality of education provided to the children.

The finance director controls and coordinates the money in the district. Salaries, benefits, and other fringes of staff; ordering materials and supplies; funding for all programs; application for and use of grant money; worker's compensation cases; and a multitude of other areas are within the financial director's purview. Few things can get an administrator into trouble more quickly than anything having to do with money. Principals should remember that even the innocent misuse of public funds, inaccurate reporting, or seemingly insignificant use of discretionary funds can result in disciplinary action or their suspension or dismissal. Money talks, and misuse of money talks loudly.

THE BUDGET PROCESS

Approaches to budget controls within districts vary widely. More emphasis has been given recently to site-based management and, thus, building-based budget control. In this approach the building (site) principal is responsible and accountable for the allocation of money to departments, grade levels, school-wide projects, equipment, curriculum material, and facilities. Staffing, utilities, and district-wide curriculum issues often are handled by central office personnel because they are difficult to relate directly to individual buildings. The goal of site-based management is determining each building's per pupil cost and utilizing funds to meet their needs.

In many schools the principal works with staff to decide the needs of the building for the coming school year. Usually this is done in the fall to allow for time to request, budget, prioritize, and order supplies before the next school year. Before any new budget process begins, an inventory should be conducted of the number of existing textbooks, paper on hand, student enrollment projections, and curriculum needs. Before you know where you are going, you have to know where you are.

To help reduce mistakes, plans must be made outlining the steps in the process. One possible flow chart might be as follows.

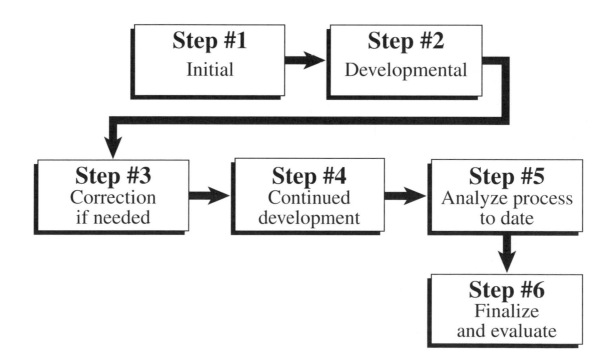

Normally, principals divide their school by teams, grades, or departments for budget purposes. These teams, groups of teachers, determine the needs, prioritize their requests, and list specific information related to ordering. This stage may take two to three weeks. Remind teachers early in the school year to kept track of upcoming needs. After the individual groups have submitted their requests for funds, the principal must decide what areas he or she will fund through the budget. Occasionally the principal has a total school budget figure in mind. He or she may have been allotted a certain amount to work with or use a zero-based budget system. In a zero-based system, no specific allotments are made, and requests for funding must be accompanied by a supporting rationale. This often results in the principal returning requests to the staff to make the cuts necessary to stay within budget guidelines.

Whatever the approach, the principal is responsible for deciding what is funded in his or her individual building. Hard decisions must be made because most requests for funds are worthwhile. Principals may choose to spend allocations in one department one year and then support another department the next year.

A typical budget, including areas often found in a typical elementary site with 600 students and 45 staff follows.

ITEM	BUDGETED
Contracted Services Social Studies	$ 265
Contracted Services Music	680
Piano tuning, speakers on new curriculum	
Postage	1,000
Mailing	
Teacher Conferences	800
Registration, mileage, and lodging for conferences	
Laminating Film	690
Roll for teacher use	
Arts and Crafts General Bid	10,781
General supplies for entire school (paper, classroom items), all materials used in teaching and learning process	
Computer Supplies	2,575
Toners, ribbons, discs, items under $50	
Day Care Supplies	1,360
Paper, games, supplies	
New Day Care Equipment	1,000
For use in day care rooms	
Teaching Supplies—Kindergarten	1,910
Teaching Supplies—Language Arts	1,123
Teaching Supplies—Art	509
Teaching Supplies—Math	817
Teaching Supplies—Science	873
Teaching Supplies—Social Studies	2,279
Teaching Supplies—Physical Ed	1,230
Teaching Supplies—Music	1,458
Meals and Refreshments	300
Refreshments for faculty meetings, parent conferences	

ITEM	BUDGETED
Textbooks—Art	87
Textbooks—Language Arts	7,372
Textbooks—Math	4,475
Textbooks—Science	2,450
Textbooks—Social Studies	5,320
Replacement Furniture	205
Business Supplies	29
For keyboarding	
Audiovisual Supplies	299
Audiotapes, videotapes, batteries, items under $50	
Audiovisual Replacement Equipment	2,920
Overhead, televisions, VCRs on a piece for piece basis	
Library Supplies	130
Library Books	4,600

Of course, every school develops a budget that reflects the needs of that particular building.

Once decisions are made, the site-based budget is added to the district-wide budget system for approval by the school board. The school board may decide to accept the recommended budget; reject it and return it to the administration for further cuts; or consider each item, line by line, and make cuts(with, one hopes, input from each building's principal). It is always best to allow the staff to make cuts in their individual areas. Problems may arise if school boards approve ordering supplies that are not those most needed by the individual building.

As indicated on the following PERT chart, steps must be taken to assure the process gathers input from all aspects of the school team.

BUDGET PROCESS

PERT Chart

In addition to the items included in the budget above, principals need to be concerned with wear and tear on facilities, computers, and other electrical equipment, and furniture, as well as preventive maintenance. A lack of attention to today's small problems may result in expensive attention to the same problems in the future.

Actually, the budget process is constantly in motion. As soon as one budget is passed by the school board, the principal and staff should begin to itemize needs for the next year's budget. Keeping an ongoing list of needs makes budget time less painful and more accurate.

PRIORITIES

Principals must prioritize continually. During the budget process, it is crucial for principals to rank items needed for quality instruction in their buildings. Input from staff and perhaps parent groups and students is helpful, but the final decisions rest with the principal. In site-based management the principal must involve the staff in the budget process. The teachers are in the best position to know what is needed for instruction. They are the individuals who should develop the rationale needed to support budget requests at the school board level.

Consultation with staff, district curriculum specialists, department heads, and other key individuals can be a great asset when determining the materials needed for each program. Their suggestions are vital and should top the list of items to be ordered. Following those items "required" for basic instruction, all materials and supplies needed to supplement the curriculum should be ordered. Third in line are materials to enhance the curriculum. At the same time, principals must be aware of several categories of needs in the building. Areas to consider include capital improvements, furniture needs, audiovisual equipment, supplies to maintain school equipment (computer discs, printer ink, audio tapes), and money set aside for unexpected circumstances.

When two equally deserving programs compete for limited funds, principals might consider alternating years, dividing the money equally, or researching additional outside funding.

SCHOOL BOARDS AND THEIR AGENDAS

Public service has been called the rent we pay for the space we occupy on Earth. Public service is a noble and worthy calling, but some board members, while publicly expressing this view, may have private agendas that reflect pressure from special interest groups. Hidden agendas that represent a minority viewpoint are not always in the best interests of all children. Some board members are elected to the board with one or two such objectives in mind. Changing discipline codes, altering athletic requirements, increasing financial support for musical programs, or removing some administrative position may be an individual's goal and, thus, may become a major political issue.

There is no doubt that taxpayers' negative feelings often are focused on the administration and, in particular, on the superintendent, who is the most visual spokesperson for the district. In extreme situations the superintendent can become totally ineffective when opposed by a coalition of board members seeking his or her removal. It is often the case, however, that once on the board, these same individuals reexamine why they ran for the board or learn, by necessity, to work within the system for the benefit of the entire district. When new board members grow like this, it helps them realize that the board sets the tone and direction for the district, and they must work in harmony with the administration if real progress is to be made.

If individual board members attempt to micromanage administrative tasks, a continual struggle may develop. Fortunately, the view of district concerns and problems from the perspective of a seat on the board alters opinions in many cases and results in a collegial approach to problem solving. This does not mean that all board members will support district administrative positions at all times and will not have alternate suggestions concerning proper policy administration. To the contrary, the more experienced the board member, the more he or she will think independently, whether in support of or in opposition to administrative recommendations and procedures. Blind rejection of opposing views and in-depth micromanagement of administrative tasks and duties are what harms district progress. Board members involved in the application of policy can undermine the efforts and frustrate staff.

One of the most difficult aspects of being a board member is convincing other board members of one's views. This is a particular problem in some areas where board members are elected by an organized pressure group. Some members may not not deviate from the position advocated by their supporters, despite arguments presented by fellow board members. The general public seldom becomes embroiled in school-based issues unless they have to do with changing boundaries, new construction, closing buildings, or pay increases. In such incidents, board members often reflect the opinions of their friends and supporters.

Certainly, running for and serving on a school board is often a frustrating and thankless job. But the desire to improve education for young people and/or maintain or reduce school taxes is enough to draw willing candidates for board openings. Some educators might welcome boards that include professional educators who might look more favorably on increased pay and educational reform. However, the public has a right to school boards that represent community interest, without a special interest bias of any kind. Individuals serving on school boards must be guardians of the public's financial support and, at the same time quality educational programs.

POLICIES

All schools have policies, which are rules passed by the local school board to regulate operation of the district. Policies may address weapons, student behavior, drug abuse, dress codes, use of technology, attendance, sexual harassment, and busing. These policies are to be enforced by the building principals under the leadership of district administrators. Policies are the basis upon which individual school rules and regulations are built.

An example of a school board policy pertaining to student searches follows.

SAMPLE SCHOOL BOARD POLICY

Section: Pupils
Title: Searches
Adopted: February 21, 1983
Revised: November 16, 1998
226.0 General Searches

Purpose

Students have the right to be secure in their person and property against unreasonable search and seizure. However, the responsibility for operating the program of the School District as safely and efficiently as possible may, on occasion, require that searches be conducted by either school officials or duly authorized law enforcement officers.

Authority

The Board and the District while willing to provide students a secure place to store their school materials and personal property, do not relinquish exclusive control of the locker/storage areas, which are provided purely for the convenience of the students. A student's use of school lockers or other locker areas is a privilege, not a right. All lockers are and shall remain the property of the School District. Accordingly, students shall have no expectation of privacy in their lockers/storage areas. The Board reserves the right to authorize its employees to inspect any and all lockers/storage areas at any time for any reason.

The building administrator or his or her designee is authorized to search a student, a student's personal possessions, or a student's motor vehicle parked on school property when there is reasonable suspicion that the student is violating Board policy or school rules or poses a threat to him/herself or the school population. This violation can be based upon evidence found on the student him/herself, within the student's personal possessions, or in the student's motor vehicle.

In the case of an exceptional student, the Superintendent shall take all necessary steps to comply with the Individuals with Disabilities Education Act, in accordance with Chapters 14 & 15 of the Pennsylvania School Code relating to students with disabilities.

Delegation

The Superintendent shall develop procedures to implement this policy. The building administrators shall be responsible for implementation of this policy at their respective level. While students have no reason to expect privacy in their lockers with regard to incursions by School District officials, students are encouraged to keep their assigned lockers closed and locked against incursion by other students.

Search Procedures in General

All requests or suggestions for a search shall be directed to the building administrator.

Before to a search, the student shall be notified and given an opportunity to be present. However, whenever the search is prompted by the reasonable suspicion of an emergency, the building administrator may conduct the search as soon as it is necessary to do so to discharge his/her duty properly to protect the persons and property in the school.

The building administrator or his/her designee and a witness shall be present whenever a search is conducted.

Searches conducted by the administrator may include but not be limited to use of certified drug dogs, metal detection units, or any device used to protect the health, safety, and welfare of the school population.

The building administrator or his/her designee shall be responsible for the safekeeping and proper disposal of any prohibited substance, object, or material found in any type of search.

At the start of the school year, each student shall be notified of this search policy.

Locker/Storage Area Searches

Students will be notified that they have no expectation of privacy in their locker/storage areas, and they will be notified that their assigned lockers/storage areas are subject to search by school officials at any time and for any reason. All locker combinations and/or duplicate keys must be kept on file in the main office. Students must not change lockers or locks without permission of the building administrator or his/her designee.

The building administrator or his/her designee shall open a student's locker for inspection by a law enforcement officer only on presentation of a duly authorized search warrant or on the intelligently and voluntarily given consent of the student.

The building administrator or his/her designee shall promptly record in writing each locker/storage area inspection. This record shall include the reason(s) for the search, persons present, objects found, and the disposition of those objects.

Motor Vehicle Searches

The building administrator or his/her designee, with an employee of the school district as a witness, may search a student's motor vehicle parked on school property when there is reasonable suspicion that the student is violating Board policy or school rules or poses a threat to him/herself or the school population, and when it is reasonable to believe that evidence of this violation can be found inside the student's motor vehicle.

In the event that a visual inspection indicates the presence of illegal articles or articles that are deemed to constitute a threat to the health, welfare, or safety of students or staff, the police shall be notified immediately and the motor vehicle may be searched.

Searches of Students and/or the Personal Possessions of Students

The building administrator or his/her designee may search a student or a student's personal possessions (items such as, but not limited to, pockets, wallets, purses, and backpacks) when there is reasonable suspicion that the student is violating Board policy or school rules or poses a threat to him/herself or the school population, and when it is reasonable to believe that evidence of this violation can be found among the student's personal possessions.

All searches will be conducted in a manner that is consistent with the purpose of the search and will not be excessively intrusive in light of the age or gender of the student and the nature of the suspected offense.

Building principals' suggestions should be acknowledged when policies are being considered, because they are ultimately responsible for enforcement. Attention must be given to the maturity level of children within the educational organization. It should be recognized that some policies may not be equally enforceable at the elementary and secondary level—i.e., harassment or name calling. In this respect, policies often allow for discretion at the building level regarding the degree of consequences. Kindergarten children are often treated differently from sixth graders because of the differences in their maturity level. As long as consistency is maintained across the district at each educational level, discretion should not become a problem.

The individual school, with the support of these policies, forms local rules that pertain to the individual school or classroom. While some freedom is allowed within most policies, the fact that the Board of Education has approved policies adds strength to enforcement and consistency in their application. Principals must remember that the School Board creates the policies and the administration carries them out. Just as School Board members should not micromanage the schools, the administration should only recommend district policy. Once decided, the policies guide further action. When schools are involved in legal action, adhering to district policy adds support. Principals need to remember that once a policy is enacted, principals who disregard its implementation or fail to enforce its intent are open to disciplinary action. In addition, principals who do not follow district policies may interfere with future legal findings and jeopardize the district position.

CHAPTER 7

SAFETY IN THE SCHOOLS

School security is one of the most pressing concerns today.

The principal must be prepared for the unexpected.

A security-minded staff is the best defense against critical incidents.

Realistic drills should be conducted to streamline and rehearse procedures.

SECURITY

One of the most pressing concerns of today's principal is the security of the school building and the safety of staff and students. This aspect of school administration, once of little concern, is a critical issue today.

The list of security concerns in today's schools is long, and principals need to be aware of and concerned about all of them. The wise principal should answer the following questions, and if the answers are no or I don't know, he or she should seek further information.

- Is the school board concerned and supportive of security efforts?
- Are you continually working toward a positive school climate?
- Is there a good working relationship with local police and fire departments?
- Are there written policies related to security?
- Is the school building clean, well-maintained, and properly supervised?
- Is the community aware of the efforts to improve security?
- Is the district planning proactively rather than waiting to react to crisis?
- Is the school emergency phone chain updated every year?
- Is there a system for students and parents to alert the district about potential dangers?
- Are staff members certified in CPR/first aid and does the principal know who they are?
- Do teachers supervise the hallways?
- Have arrangements been made to evaluate the school to an alternate facility?
- Does the principal know the location of all utility and alarm shutoffs?
- Are all weather alert radios continually on?
- Does the student handbook include safety procedures and policies?
- Do peer mediation procedures exist, and are students aware of this means to avoid violent confrontations?
- Is the building facility clear of shrubs, trees and other obstructions to provide a clear view?

- Are entry doors (one door per building for visitors) monitored by personnel, camera, or electronic entry systems?
- Does the school have immediate communication access to all other buildings and the central office?
- Does the school have an alternate public address system such as bullhorns?
- Do office phones have Caller I.D. installed (in the event of bomb threats)?
- Does each classroom have a phone or call button to communicate with the office?
- Is a system in place to control and monitor after-school activities?

Answers to these questions and others may demonstrate a need for strategic planning. As more incidents involving security occur in public schools, the pressure increases on the principal to have a well-developed plan to avoid and, if all else fails, react to critical incidents in the school building.

CRITICAL INCIDENT PLAN

The school principal must be prepared for the unexpected. Defending the school from violence, once unique to some inner city schools, has been extended to schools at every level and in all segments of society. Today's principals face the dilemma of creating a safe place for children to learn and employees to work, while maintaining an open, friendly environment conducive to learning. Unfortunately, it is now the principal's responsibility to plan for the unexpected, prepare for the unthinkable, and ensure that everything that can be done, is done, in case of an emergency. The rise in school violence and intrusions into the school building have increased the need for principals to develop a *critical incident plan*, to deal with what once was considered too be unthinkable. A partial list of critical incidents for which the principals must prepare includes:

- bomb threats
- gas leaks
- suicide attempts
- snipers outside the building
- weapons in the building
- severe weather
- hostage situations
- hazardous material spills
- kidnapping
- vehicle accidents
- armed intruders
- bus incidents

These threats to the safety of the students and staff are major concerns, and it is incumbent on prudent administrators to lobby proactively for corrective action where deficiencies are discovered. The need for a comprehensive, user-friendly plan to meet these challenges has never been greater, and a secure building is less likely to be compromised.

THE SCHOOL BUILDING

Every school is unique. Principals preparing a Critical Incident Plan (CIP) need to answer a variety of questions:

- Can all classroom doors be locked from the inside?
- Do communications exist between each classroom to the office?
- Are exterior doors routinely locked during school hours to prevent entry?
- Do stand-by staff know where to report when needed?
- Are code words (for this type of emergency) clearly understood?
- Is there a sign-in procedure and badge system for all visitors?
- Are all employees required to wear I.D. badges?
- Is there a panic communication system between the school and police?
- Do principals carry cell phones at all times?
- Is there a backup plan for absent or incapacitated leadership?
- Are bus drivers routinely briefed by police on what to do in hostage situations?
- Do office phones have Caller I.D.?
- Is peer mediation emphasized to reduce conflict?
- Have staff members been trained in CPR and first aid?
- Are isolated areas screened by security cameras?
- Are backpacks eliminated during the school day?
- Should school buses be equipped with video cameras?
- Are metal detectors used at dances and after-school events?
- Is the entrance to events reduced to a single location?

Whether or not these conditions exist, principals in individual buildings must develop and implement plans to increase the safety of all staff and students. Where possible, steps should be initiated to establish security committees, employ security consultants, and budget for safety improvements.

CHECK WITH POLICE

Local police agencies, fire departments and ambulance services are a critical resource for the principal. Working with the police tactical unit and bomb squad can prove very beneficial when formulating plans. Local police and fire departments need maps of the school and should meet on a regular basis to review emergency procedures. SWAT units should conduct drills with school staff, when school is not in session, to raise security awareness. But, despite police/fire cooperation and involvement, until these people arrive, the initial reaction of principals can save lives and greatly aid in crisis resolution.

INVOLVE TEACHERS

Staff involvement in planning, implementation, and practice of critical incident drills is vitally important. A well-educated staff is the best defense against a critical incident becoming a tragedy. The staff must realize the seriousness of the CIP and the need for drills to avoid misinformation, clarify procedures, and assess plans. Realistic drills should be held periodically throughout the year to streamline procedures and increase understanding of security measures.

PRELIMINARY STEPS IN CIP DEVELOPMENT

All district emergency material (booklets, policies, and guidelines) should be reviewed before the school's CIP is written. Attention to school board policy and administrative guidelines will provide guidance and support decisions, and while most aspects of the CIP are site-based, an overall district security plan is a necessity. Principals who have central office and board support are in a much stronger position to formulate plans and make critical decisions. Specific plans should be developed, as well, for individual facilities, taking into consideration the unique aspects of each site. District-supported plans give parents needed reassurance that schools take security seriously and that safety is more important than convenience.

USING THE CIP MANUAL

Once prepared, the CIP manual must be readily available and user-friendly. But remember that emergencies allow little time for reading a reference manual, the booklet must serve only as a quick reference for well-established, rehearsed procedures. All staff, including traveling and itinerant teachers and support personnel, must be fully aware of their role in the case of an emergency. The plan should outline the responsibility and immediate course of action for all school personnel, including the administrator, secretaries, custodians, and teachers. Backup personnel should be designated to assume the leadership role in the event that the principal is out of the building or incapacitated.

CIP CONTENTS

Depending upon their individual building circumstances, principles should consider the following in developing a critical incident plan for their schools.

- Develop a plan that calls attention to the incident for staff without alarming students.
- Make certain all code words and critical instructions are clearly understood.
- Establish a plan where all staff not supervising students report to a central point.
- Have a crisis response team in place and well trained.
- Notify the Central Office about all emergencies.
- Be accountable for all students and staff in emergencies.
- Supply police/fire agencies with maps of the school building.
- Organize a plan and location to meet the media representatives.
- Have walkie-talkies available.

- Check flashlights often and keep extra batteries on hand.
- Have emergency kits available (first aid, blood pathogen kits).
- Increase staff visibility before and after school and between classes.
- Set up a hotline or drop box for reports of school violence.
- Hold CIP drills at least twice a year.
- Building exteriors should be well lighted and free of high shrubbery.

Principals have primarily responsibility for security of their buildings. Having a fast, immediate resource available to assist staff in dealing with critical incidents can help avoid escalating dangerous situations pending the arrival of the official emergency personnel. While principals cannot always avoid critical incidents, efforts to create well-established safety procedures and a well-developed critical incident plan can help.

CRISIS INTERVENTION TEAMS

Regardless of the steps taken in any school during a crisis, or the existence of a well-thought-out critical incident plan, when a crisis occurs, follow-up activities or a postintervention response is necessary. A disaster, violent act, or sudden death of a student or staff member is an intensely emotional event in the life of a school. Students and staff are greatly affected by such a crisis, and the school, often the place where they hear of the crisis, has an obligation to work with those affected to help in the healing process. Students react in many different ways to crisis and stress and feel a sense of loss or anger for as long as two years. There is also the danger of another crisis if student reactions are not dealt with effectively. In the event of a crisis before school opens, the school must:

- obtain all factual information
- meet with staff before the students arrive
- review plans to greet the students and permit student discussion
- permit concerned students to seek adult counsel during the day
- prepare a written notice concerning the crisis to send home with students
- meet with staff at the end of the day to review procedures
- continue to monitor and support the staff
- arrange for additional counseling for staff and students

In the event of a critical incident during the school day (the most difficult to deal with), after the incident is confirmed, care must taken to notify the staff immediately through a written memo. This short memo should be distributed to all staff with instructions to read it to students as soon as possible. The memo might be similar to the following:

> This morning at 9:35, James Gribbon, a seventh-grade student in our school, was seriously injured in our industrial arts classroom. James's parents were called while Nurse Brown responded to the emergency. When the ambulance arrived, James was taken to Metro Hospital, where he was listed in serious condition. I know all of you are concerned about James. We will keep you informed of any updates regarding his condition.

The memo is intended to inform the staff and students, avoid rumors, and reduce any misinformation that might be communicated to parents and the community. Principals must be careful to state just facts and not include extensive details or assumptions. Students should be kept in the classrooms for a period of time, but any students showing signs of distress should be sent to the office with a classmate. Depending on the incident, principals should resume the normal school routine as soon as possible.

The Crisis Response Team, following a predesigned crisis plan, should draft a notice to send home to parents at dismissal. In this notice, in addition to providing factual information, the principal should reassure the parents that the situation is under control, that the school continues to be a safe place, and that their children are safe. Parents should be asked not to call the school, and should be told that future notices will be forthcoming.

Staff should report for a short meeting after school for an update on the situation and an assessment of student reactions during the school day. The following morning there should be a staff meeting before school begins to discuss any special procedures for the day. Staff should be sensitive to any students that may need counseling.

Principals need to remember after-school programs, be aware of students riding buses, and alert before-school programs the following morning.

The principal must take an active role in helping students and the school community deal with a crisis. To meet this goal, well-established procedures must be carried out by well-organized and trained staff. These procedures also must be communicated to resources outside the school district long before they are needed to increase their effectiveness during a crisis.

The school is the common place where children first gather after a crisis. It is the principal's responsibility to have a Crisis Response Team in place to deal with any trauma and stress and to intervene to reduce the emotional impact. While many outside agencies can be involved, the school principal and staff are the first lines of defense for meeting any emergency. Principals must make certain their staffs are well trained and must practice the procedures necessary to respond to such events regularly.

CHAPTER 8

THE NUTS AND BOLTS OF ADMINISTRATION

*Substitute teachers are expected to fulfill all of
the responsibilities of regular teachers.*

*Excluding students from special classes should
never be used as a punishment.*

Special teachers should be scheduled for all regularly assigned duties.

Without team planning, there is no true teamwork.

EXPECTATIONS FOR SUBSTITUTE TEACHERS

The substitute is expected to assume the responsibilities of the classroom teacher, maintain the classroom routine, retain a professional image throughout the day, and try to keep the instructional level and learning experiences as uninterrupted as possible.

Substitutes normally are expected to:

- Arrive at the indicated school on time
- Report to the principal's office on arrival, where specific instruction peculiar to the school is available (classroom number, keys, etc.)
- Upon arrival in the classroom:
  — Locate Plan Book/Lesson Plans
  — Assign duties for the day (bus, wardrobe, etc.)
  — Look for the Substitute Folder (usually in the middle desk drawer)
  — The Substitute Folder should contain most of the following:
    – location of Plan Book/Lesson Plans
    – daily schedule, lunch schedule, bus and recess duty schedule
    – any special activities or assemblies for the day
    – location of manuals
    – location of activity worksheets
    – class lists
    – class helpers
    – disciplinary methods/actions
    – reading group lists and math group lists
    – any special class rules, playground rules, school rules
    – location of any special equipment

- current seating charts
- fire drill/tornado drill exit schedule and procedures
- list of extra activities students are allowed to do
- copies of Substitute Teacher Report forms
- copies of Summary Report of a Substitute form
- identification of students with special medical problems
- critical incident plan

— Follow the plans left by the teacher, the time schedule, and the regular routine as closely as possible
— Begin with the planned opening exercise:
  - Recite the Pledge of Allegiance
  - Reading from the opening exercise book/patriotic song/silent meditation, etc.
— Take attendance, list absentees on separate paper along with any pertinent information. Send any absentee notes/excuses brought from home to the office
— In some elementary schools, especially Satellite Lunch Program schools, take an accurate student lunch and milk count each morning before lunchtime
— Refer to the principal for any special instructions for fire drills, movement through the halls, cafeteria and rainy day procedures, etc.
— Leave the room in order, with most written work corrected and on the teacher's desk
— Realize that there are individual differences in teachers and their teaching methods, and in pupils and their learning
— Look to the principal for any help and guidance; all teachers, regular and substitute, are under his or her immediate supervision
— Maintain good professional ethics, and avoid critical comments of pupils, parents, and personnel, in school and the community
— Be in control of the situation at all times, but avoid such punishments as:
  - Making a child write a word, phrase, or sentence repeatedly
  - Making the child perform a physical act to the point of exhaustion
  - Ridiculing the child.
  - Using the halls to isolate the child
  - Depriving the child of lunch or participation in special classes (i.e., art, music, physical education) or any other academic subject
— Use a positive approach when dealing with a child's problems; praise what is good far more than you criticize what is bad
— Use common sense always; most rules, regulations, guides, and directives in the world are no substitute
— Keep your sense of humor because every problem is not a tragedy; if you have no sense of humor, try to develop one
— Before the substitute teacher leaves for the day:
  - Fill out the Summary Report of an Elementary Substitute and take it to the office
  - Check with the office secretary or principal to see if you are needed the next day

SCHEDULING SPECIAL CLASSES

Special teachers have a unique situation because they meet a variety of students throughout the school day, unlike elementary homeroom teachers who usually meet a more consistent group. When creating a special schedule (art, music, library, physical education), allow preparation time between special periods. The art teacher may need time to clean up, put away ceramics material, and get paints out for the next period; the music teacher might need to rearrange the room for the next class; the physical education teacher may need to store equipment and prepare for incoming students. Whenever possible, the principal should try to schedule grade levels in sequence. When the art teacher has a first grade, a fourth grade, a first grade, a fifth grade, and then a second grade, extensive rearrangement of supplies and material is necessary. While scheduling grade levels in sequence is not always possible, consultation with special teachers before the schedule is created can be beneficial to everyone.

Conflicts sometimes may arise between academic and special teachers. The wise principal makes it clear that all subjects are important. Consequently, punishment should never include the exclusion of a student from a special class to make up academic work, nor should a special teacher hold a student out of an academic class for disciplinary reasons.

While there are many approaches to scheduling special classes, a matrix is often helpful. In this type of scheduling, each special class is listed across the top of a sheet. Time slots are aligned below each special for all of the sections to be assigned. Care must be taken to place each section in each special time slot.

SAMPLE SPECIALS SCHEDULE

SPECIALS SCHEDULE 2000 – 2001

MONDAY	ART	MUSIC	P.E.
9:25 – 10:00	PETERSON	SULLIVAN	
10:00 – 10:35	HOWLAND	ELWELL	Phy. HANDICAP
10:40 – 11:15	*DALY*	MERZ	BECK
11:20 – 11:55		FULLER	WASHEK
12:40 – 1:15	PUTNAM	MILLER	ANDERSON
1:20 – 1:50	SCULLY	KUHOLSKI	HIGGINS
1:55 – 2:30	MILLER	ANDERSON	BROWN
2:35 – 3:10	KING		PUTNAM
TUESDAY			
9:25 – 10:00	WELSH	PETERSON	SULLIVAN
10:00 – 10:35	MERZ	HOWLAND	ELWELL
10:40 – 11:15		WILLIAMS	MERZ
11:20 – 11:55	WASHEK		FULLER
12:40 – 1:15	ANDERSON	WIDGER	MILLER
1:20 – 1:50	KUHOLSKI	HIGGINS	
1:55 – 2:30	HIGGINS	ROBINSON	KUHOLSKI
2:35 – 3:10	BROWN	*DALY*	SCHOLL
WEDNESDAY			
9:25 – 10:00	FULLER		KING
10:00 – 10:35	WILLIAMS	SCULLY	WELSH
10:40 – 11:15	BECK	CHORUS	WILLIAMS
11:20 – 11:55	ZACKS	CHORUS	
12:40 – 1:15	WIDGER	SCHOOL B	SCHOOL C
1:20 – 1:50		SCHOOL B	SCHOOL C
1:55 – 2:30	ROBINSON	SCHOOL B	SCHOOL C
2:35 – 3:10	SCHOLL	SCHOOL B	SCHOOL C
THURSDAY	No Specials classes on Thursday		
FRIDAY			
9:25 – 10:00	SULLIVAN	KING	PETERSON
10:00 – 10:35	ELWELL	WELSH	HOWLAND
10:40 – 11:15		BECK	SCULLY
11:20 – 11:55		WASHEK	ADAPT
12:40 – 1:15	SCHOOL B		WIDGER
1:20 – 1:50	SCHOOL B	REHEARSAL	*DALY*
1:55 – 2:30	SCHOOL B	BROWN	ROBINSON
2:35 – 3:10	SCHOOL B	SCHOLL	ZACKS

Additionally, staff normally prefer that primary classes not be interrupted in the morning. Principals also must be careful to avoid a lunch period conflict, or avoid scheduling two specials for an individual student on a single day whenever possible. It is usually best to draft special schedules in the spring so that staff can review them and point out any perceived problems. After the principal makes any necessary changes, the schedule is ready for the fall session.

Special schedules often are unique to each school building. The length of the periods and the number of classes a week for each child depend on the number of classrooms in the school, the extent that special teachers are shared with other schools, and the number of other academic classes in the normal school day. In any event, principals should try to allow as much time as possible for special classes because these hands-on activities typically require extra time to complete assigned tasks. If extended periods are not possible, planning additional class periods for some advanced classes is beneficial.

At the same time, principals should schedule special teachers for all regularly assigned school duties. There normally is no legitimate reason why special teachers cannot be assigned bus, hall, wardrobe, locker, or playground duty. The fact that they are not responsible for homerooms, and thus do not have routine duties as regular teachers, makes such assignments reasonable and fair.

CLASS SIZE

Many teachers are concerned about class size because they feel it affects their instructional success. They feel, and justifiably so, that the more students in their classes, the more discipline problems, the more extra time for special help, the more homework and tests to grade, and the more stress they experience. While any competent principal tries to balance class sizes among the teaching staff, sometimes this is impossible, since the number of incoming students, especially during the school year, exceeds desired class size. Staff must understand that this situation is often beyond the principal's ability to correct. Often there is no additional funding for new teachers, so class size increases. Perhaps creative scheduling or reassigning staff may ameliorate the situation. More often than not, it will correct the matter only temporarily. If an increase in enrollment is forecast, the principal should seek the central office's help in obtaining additional staff to meet the school's changing needs. However, hiring additional educational assistants can help the classroom teacher deal with larger classes temporarily. While the principal should try to obtain the needed professional staff, educational assistants are less expensive and, in some cases, more acceptable to budget-conscience school boards.

LEARNING STYLES

Children learn in different ways. While it would be beneficial to assign students with certain learning styles to teachers with similar teaching styles, that usually is not possible. To do this individual students' learning styles and individual teachers' teaching styles would have to be determined. Additionally, assigning students to teachers based on learning and teaching styles does not guarantee academic success. But identifying student learning styles can help the teacher to plan class activities because many of them can be designed with the students' style in mind. Teachers can be assigned projects that highlight their talents and better meet their learning styles.

FLEXIBILITY OF GROUPS

One approach to help meet the needs of students is to create flexible groupings. Such groupings make it possible to reassign students to subgroups depending on their abilities. For example, a child might be assigned to (or select) a high math group and a lower-level reading group. In contrast, homogeneous groups can be formed to allow students of similar ability to learn together and progress at their own rate. This type of grouping, sometimes called *tracking*, can have negative results. Some children may begin to feel they are in the "slow" or "dummy" group, and others feel they are the "gifted" or "smart" kids. Many teachers feel that it is easier to prepare for and instruct these groups, because the entire class moves as a whole with little variation in presentation. Also, slower classes can be given remedial help as a group, and high-achieving students are not held back by slower students.

In contrast to homogenous ability grouping is heterogenous grouping that allows a mixture of abilities in each class. This approach permits more academically oriented students to serve as models for at-risk students and projects a more realistic view of the world. However, many feel it is more difficult to teach a class of mixed abilities, and some teachers may focus lessons toward the middle of the group, thus not challenging the high achievers or providing for the at-risk students. If heterogeneous grouping is followed, classes, such as those for the gifted, can provide additional enrichment for academically advanced students, and remedial classes can help those at risk.

LESSON PLANS

Poor teachers seldom have outstanding lesson plans. In fact, teachers who have difficulties in their classes often are poorly prepared. Regular review of weekly lesson plans allows principals to monitor teacher planning, adherence to curriculum, and proper sequence of lessons. Evidence of failure to plan may indeed be evidence of planning to fail.

Two good examples of lesson plans, one for an academic class and one for a physical education class, are portrayed as follows.

LANGUAGE ARTS

STORY: Mule & Ann Thunder

Unit 4 Plan 4	READING	WRITE	GRAMMAR	SPELLING	
MONDAY Seatwork D.L.P. JOURNAL	9:35 TO 10:40 BREAK AT 11:55 • Create a Community of Learners T: 144–145 Transparency #14	PRES. REPORTS	D.L.P R: 15 • Wkbk. pages	Spelling pre-Test T: 167 3 × each for ones missed	CORRECT WKBK. FROM FRIDAY MUSIC 10:06–10:40
TUESDAY D.L.P. JOURNAL	9:30 TO 11:20 BREAK AT 11:05 • Build Background T: 146 Transparency #15 • Develop Vocab T: 147 Wkbk. p.34	PRES. REPORTS	D.L.P R: 15 GRAMMAR REVIEW	• Teach words T: 167 Spell wksht.	GYM 10:05–10:40
WEDNESDAY D.L.P. JOURNAL	9:30 TO 11:40 BREAK AT 11:45 • Meet the Author T: 149 • Intro to story • Begin reading story T: 150–161	PRES. REPORTS ART 11:25–12:00	D.L.P R: 15 • Teach Grammar Lesson #1 T: 166 and Wksht. #43	• Teach words T: 167 • Alpha order and/or sentences	• Intro to Key Strategy T: 153 SEQUENCE SPANISH 11:30
THURSDAY D.L.P. JOURNAL	9:30 TO 11:20 • FINISH STORY AND DISCUSS CD ROM ROOM 9:30–10:30	PRES. REPORTS KEYBOARDING 11:10–11:35	• Teach Grammar Lesson #2 T: 166 and Wksht. #44	• Teach words T: 167 • Worksheet	• Teach and track skill through reading T: 150–161 Wkbk. p.37 & 40 Transparency #17
FRIDAY D.L.P. JOURNAL	9:30 TO 10:40 • Reread story & do Revisits T: 150–161 • Check Comprehension T: 162 Wkbk. p.35 COMPUTER LAB 11:00–12:00	PRES. REPORTS	D.L.P R: 15	• Spell post-test T: 167	• Review skill and transfer to new text T: 170–173 Wkbk. pgs.38–41

LESSON PLANS   **WEEK OF:** MARCH 5–9, 2001

MATH 12:00 – 12:55		SOCIAL STUDIES
6WBT DISPLAY COMPETENCY of Ch. 5		
		1:50–2:30 (Washeski) and 2:30–3:10 (Fuller)
• Correct P.O.D. • Students take the Ch. 5 Test HW = Book p. 245		• WATCH SPANISH (2 SHOWS BEHIND)
Explore Mult. patterns for 2 × 2 mult.		REVIEW CH. 4 FOR QUIZ
• Book pp. 250–251 – orally • Wkbk. p. 6-1 • Correct and reteach if necessary HW = Wksht. 6-1		• Play review game for Quiz HW = Study for quiz
Estimate products with 2 digit factors		Display competency of Ch. 4 through a quiz
• Correct HW and POD • Book pp. 252–253 • Do and correct together HW = Wksht. 6-2		• Students take the Chapter 4 quiz • Complete Map Scale Activity sheet HW = Finish Wksht.
Multiply by Multiples of 10		Explain how French and Indian War affected PA
• Correct HW and POD • Book pp. 254–255 HW = Wksht. 6-3		• Correct HW • Go over tests • Read and discuss book pp. 106–109 • Take notes and make new folders
Explore multiplying with 2 digit factors		**TEAM MATH TIME**
• Correct HW and POD • Book pp. 256–257 . . . do problems at board • Wkbk. p 6-4		**PSSA** **REVIEW**

LUNCH 1:00 TO 1:30   AND   RECESS 1:35 TO 1:50

ACTIVITY—FITNESS STATIONS/V-SIT
Week of 3/5–3/9
Grades K–5

Goal
To test one fitness component, flexibility, while developing various physical skills (see specific objectives at each station).

Introduction
Today's fitness Test V-sit
The flexed arm hang measures our upper body strength and endurance. This is not a contest but a skill you try to do your best. Students will be placed in small groups of 4–5 people. Rotation at station will occur approximately every 5 minutes. Poor behavior at station will result in time out with me working on written work.

Exercise Spots
Students follow a series of jumping jacks (warm-up), stretches, crunches, and push-ups to improve overall fitness.

Fitness Station #1
Objective—To measure flexibility in hamstrings and back muscles.
Performing the Test: Student removes shoes, and sits on floor with legs in V position, heels fit snugly against foot stops. Student clasps thumbs so hands are together, palms down and places them on measuring strip. Student slowly reaches forward as far as possible, keeping fingers on measurement strip with feet flexed. After two practices the student holds reach for recording by teacher.

Fitness Station #2 (Bowling)
Objective—To cooperate with classmates, to develop rolling skills at a target, and to develop math skills.
One lane is set up with pins and one ball. Small groups will compete with one another for highest score. One roll per person, reset pins.

Fitness Station #3 (Basketball)
Objective—To develop shooting and dribbling skills.
Each student will be provided with their own ball to work on dribbling, shooting, and passing skills.

Fitness Station #4 (Jump roping skills/Jump the creek)
Objective—To cooperate with peers; develop jumping ability; develop coordination
Students will either work individually on single jump roping skills, together with the double long jump rope, or in small group with jump the creek. The K–2 grade will work individually on jump rope skills.

Fitness Station #5 (Volleyball)
Objective—To develop hand/eye coordination; cooperation with a small group.
Students will work together to keep the beach ball up in a game of keep up. If net is available they may use previously taught skills to play a small game of volleyball.

Class Discussion and Closure
1st and 2nd—What was out fitness test today?
3rd—What did our fitness test measure?
4th and 5th—What are some ways (exercises) to improve your fitness test score?
Equipment—V sit marker, mat, 6 basketballs (hoops), 6 short jump ropes, 1 long jump rope, floor tape, cones, volleyball net with beach ball, bowling equipment for one group.

CONFERENCES

Most principals recognize the importance of staff development. Inservice programs help to meet this need. Sometimes staff members have to attend conferences out of town. In those districts that have reduced or curtailed conferences, new approaches, initiatives, and programs are less common. Conferences are one of the few incentives that a principal can offer to staff members to reward their good work, and attending them also benefits district programs. As mentioned earlier, staff members should prepare a written report of ideas learned and, if possible, present the new information to fellow staff members.

TEAM PLANNING

In schools where there are several teachers at each grade level or where departmentalization is desired, team scheduling and team planning are critical. Teachers assigned to team, or departmental teaching, who are not provided with team planning time will not operate as true teams. Teams need to discuss and plan events that are part of the school program. Teams need to depend on the strengths of each team member and the expertise within their own grade or department. If it is not possible to schedule team planning during the day (during art, music, or physical education classes, for example), time should be arranged at the beginning or end of the school day. Principals must remember that without team planning, there is no true teamwork.

CAFETERIA

The period of time that students are in the cafeteria for lunch and, in some cases, for breakfast, demands unique rules. Lunch programs in schools help maintain students' energy level and provide a break in the school day. While the normal school rules apply (no running, throwing things, disrespect, etc.), students are allowed to talk and, in some cases, move around without direct teacher or supervisor permission. Principals must remember that this time is one of the few times during the day when students can talk to their friends and enjoy the social aspects of school. Lunch is not a free-for-all, but rather a structured, controlled period of time set aside for a specific reason. As long as reasonable and logical rules are followed, students should be permitted some freedom.

STAFF MEETINGS

The first faculty meeting of the school year can set the tone for a successful opening. While every school and school year is unique, the agenda for the first faculty meeting might look like the following.

FIRST FACULTY MEETING OF THE YEAR

1. Introduction of new/returning professional staff members
2. Teachers submit one educational goal
3. Teachers turn in team meeting schedule
4. Integrating art, music, and P.E. into the curriculum
5. Computer care
6. Check e-mail daily
7. Committee representatives
8. School goals for the year
9. Faculty meeting dates
10. All classrooms locked each night
11. All district staff must wear I.D. badges at all times
12. Nonviolent conflict resolution
13. Review critical incident plan
14. Please be at school no later than 8:20 A.M. every day
15. Parent conferences
16. Step outside classroom door when classes change, in the morning, and at dismissal to improve supervision
17. Absences other than illness
18. Classroom observations
19. Lesson plans
20. Adult lunches
21. Open house
22. School pictures
23. Taking attendance in the morning
24. Custodial concerns
25. Transportation requests
26. Use of office detention
27. Perfect attendance
28. Student discipline referrals
29. Field trips
30. Elementary report card

31. Religious holidays
32. Use of large group instructional areas
33. Summary of security measures
34. Dates to notes

Regardless of its content, the agenda should be well planned, relevant, informative, and inclusive because staff will refer to it often during the school year.

CHAPTER 9

STUDENT-RELATED ISSUES

To reduce retention, develop strategies for the at-risk learner and involve parents.

*Nothing can be achieved at a conference when
parents are angry and teachers are upset.*

*Positive reinforcement has proven to be more successful
than punishment in altering a student's behavior.*

*Create a climate where every child leaves school every day feeling that somebody
cares about him or her as a person.*

*To develop a sense of calm and security, children should
see the principal when they enter and at dismissal each day.*

RETENTION

Retention is often a controversial subject. Many primary teachers feel that some students require additional time to mature and develop before going on to the next grade. Others feel that retention and separation of students from their classmates has a negative impact on their self-esteem. To avoid holding children back in a grade, principals should concentrate extra help, develop strategies for at-risk students, solicit parents' cooperation, and monitor students' progress closely. If all of these strategies fail, and the teacher fears that the child may experience stress and failure in the next grade, and the fear exists that the child will experience frustration, retention should be considered. However, retention after the third grade is usually inappropriate. Students retained after the third grade often experience feelings of rejection, lack of self-worth, and may become disciplinary problems because they think they know the material already.

The secret to reducing retention is assessing at-risk students in-depth, developing alternative strategies, and involving parents as active participants. Only after all of these efforts have failed should retention be considered.

STUDENT RECORDS

Safe and secure maintenance of student records is an important part of the principal's responsibility. Permanent files should be secured in a location safe from unauthorized access and should only contain those records necessary for educational purposes. Some states, such as Pennsylvania, have developed guidelines for classifying student reports and records that simplify this process.

Student records must be maintained for legal and professional reasons. State laws require schools to establish policy for collecting and maintaining student grades and other information relevant to a child's education. Districts need to maintain only certain, nondiscriminatory information, and they must adhere closely to state regulations. Those items classified as "A" records include the student's name, address, Social Security number, transcript, etc. These records have to be kept for ninety-nine years after the student's high school graduation. "B" records include the individual's education plan and information for the next year's teacher to maintain the student's academic progress. These records can be purged at specific points in the educational process such as fifth, eighth, and twelfth grade. Records of weapon possession, drug, and alcohol violations are maintained until graduation. Items of immediate importance for the current year are considered "C" records. They contain current important letters, discipline records, etc. Records that continue to be important can be transferred from classification "C" to "B" and maintained longer.

Care must be taken to safeguard records against unauthorized access. Lists of those professionals allowed to read individual files should be located by the permanent file cabinet. Parents and guardians have the right to view their child's records upon request.

REPORT CARDS AND PARENT CONFERENCES

Public schools must inform parents regularly of their children's progress. Usually at six- or nine-week intervals, report cards are sent home for parents to review. Deciding on the type of report card used can be a difficult task for a district: Should grades be recorded in percentages or in letter grades? Should special subjects, such as physical education, art, and music carry the same weight as other academic courses? Should student deportment be part of the report? Regardless of the type of report card, its purpose is to inform parents and serve as a school record of courses successfully or unsuccessfully completed.

Most school systems include some method for conducting parent/teacher conferences during the school year. It is important that parents have the opportunity to meet with teachers to discuss student success and/or behavior in the classroom. While teachers and parents often meet without the principal being present, in situations where problems may arise or confrontations are likely, the principal should always attend. In cases of this nature, the principal should support the teacher, advocate for the child, and be a helpful professional for the parent. In the event of clear evidence that a teacher made an error, the principal should schedule private discussions with the staff member to correct the matter. Where student behavior is an issue, children should be told specifically the possible consequences. Principals should remind parents that their common goal is children's success in school. Parents who become upset should be reminded of this fact and asked to reschedule a meeting if tempers get the better of them. Nothing can be achieved at a meeting with angry parents and upset teachers.

INCENTIVE PROGRAMS

A school whose actions are based on positive reinforcement rather than punishment has proven to be more successful in altering student behavior. The old saying that you catch more flies more with honey than you do with vinegar is true. Consider stating rules in positive ways:

Please walk (rather than *Don't run!*)
Please stay in line (rather than *Don't cut!*)
Please raise you hands (rather than *Don't shout out!*)
Please remain quite (rather than *Don't talk!*)

Experience has shown that many students remember the last words they hear, so if someone says, "Don't run," they remember run, if someone says "Don't talk," they remember talk. We all know we respond more favorably to a smile and a gentle reminder than a frown and a scolding. Enhance your environment with positive reinforcements. Praise openly and often. Use the public address system to commend classes and individuals for good work. Set up Student of Week, Perfect Attendance, or Most Improved Student programs. Recognize students who help keep the school clean, assist others, and succeed in academics or sports. Make your school a place where kids go to feel good about themselves. Make your building a school where winning is a habit. Help teachers to spotlight student successes and, at least for a little while, make every student feel he or she has been successful.

Remember that every child has abilities and talents. While it may be true that these students' abilities, skills, and talents may not be academically oriented, they still can contribute to class discussions, help with public address announcements, and demonstrate their need to be seen and appreciated. In today's world, the school stands as one of the last places where a child can find success, recognition, and a feeling of accomplishment and belonging in a positive way. Create a climate where every child, leaves school every day with the feeling that somebody cares about him or her as a person.

ENTRY AND EXIT

As mentioned earlier, arrival at school can be a critical time of the day. This is the time to show students that the principal is in the building: his or her presence helps to develop principal/student rapport, and permits contact with bus aides, drivers, and other supervisory staff. Once this policy is established, the students expect to see the principal and will develop a feeling of security on entering the building. Students must feel secure while at school, and the principal's presence can add to that feeling of safety.

Equally important is the presence of the principal at dismissal. Students need to see the principal as they leave for the day. Comments from the principal such as, "Remember to do that homework," "Hey, be sure to zip up that coat," or "Have a great evening," lead to a heightened sense of caring in the students' eyes. Principals need to remember that a good sense of humor and a positive attitude are the key to success in dealing with students.

TRAFFIC FLOW

The procedure used at dismissal can end a busy school day peacefully or create an additional headache. Principals should study the patterns of student traffic flow and analyze their effectiveness. Avoiding interferences such as cross traffic, having all students leave through one door, allowing parents to block hallways, and confusion within groups of exiting students will ease the transition between school and the trip home. Staff should supervise hallways and exits to cut down on misbehavior.

Parents should be familiar with dismissal safety issues. Soliciting their assistance will be helpful in organizing new approaches. A committee of parents and staff looking at the vehicular traffic patterns or methods of loading buses may make suggestions that will improve the situation. Sometimes a small adjustment in dismissal time, or reversing walker dismissal and bus dismissal can affect traffic concerns.

RULES

For school rules to be effective, they must be fair and consistent. But students and parents have to perceive them as fair and consistent, as well. While school rules often reflect school district policies, every school has specific rules for safe and effective operation of the individual building.

An outline of discipline-related areas that might be included in district policy is displayed below.

INFRACTION AND CONSEQUENCES

Incident	Possible Consequences
Bomb threats	Immediate suspension pending a board hearing
Cutting class, not reporting to assigned class	One hour of detention
Disrespect for teachers, visitors, fellow classmates	Minimum of one hour of detention
Disruptive behavior, interference with instruction	Verbal reprimand to suspension
Drug and alcohol (possession, intent to deliver, paraphernalia, nonprescription drugs in sports	Suspension to referral to the board
Explosives, from small firecrackers to pipe bombs	Up to 10 days' suspension and possible referral to the board
Failure to attend detention	Increased detention hours

Incident	Possible Consequences
False fire alarms (yelling fire, pulling the alarm)	Suspension pending a board hearing
Falsifying information (forging parents' names, cheating, giving false verbal responses)	Minimum of one hour of detention
Fighting (mutual exchange of blows, attacks on others; care must be taken to define fighting as opposed to slapping, wrestling, pushing, tripping, etc.)	One to three days' suspension
Fire code violation Starting a fire, burning matches	Up to 10 days' suspension and possible referral to the board
Harassment (verbal, racial, sexual, written, etc.)	Minimum of one hour of detention
Illegal locker use (reminder that lockers are school property only if students are told)	Minimum of one hour of detention
Physical acts of aggression (lying in wait for another, deliberate attempt to hurt another)	Minimum of one day of suspension
Tardiness and unexcused tardiness (continual lateness to school)	Minimum of one hour of detention
Technology violations (damaging to computers, illegal use of the Internet, violation of others' passwords)	Loss of technology use and possible suspension
Terrorist threats and acts (threats to harm, hurt, or injure others, in person, on the phone, or in writing)	Possible suspension and referral to the board
Theft (stealing from another person, or taking school property)	Minimum of one hour of detention to suspension
Tobacco violations (lookouts, possession, on buses, in sports, in season and out)	Suspension and/or fine
Truancy (out of school without legal cause)	One hour of detention
Unexcused absence	Possible fine from local court system

Incident	Possible Consequences
Vandalism and destroying property (breaking or damaging property)	Restitution and additional consequences on a case-by-case basis
Weapons violations (possession of an instrument that is intended to do harm; this area is the basis of many zero tolerance policies)	Immediate removal from school property, suspension pending a school board hearing

In secondary schools students should be involved in developing rules. Involvement of the Student Council or other student group adds ownership and increases students' compliance. Many staff members have ideas about school rules that, while valuable, may need some adjustment because some teachers expect varying degrees of enforcement for similar infractions. For rules to be enforced, faculty should discuss them and committees, across grade levels, should have some say in formulating them. Those making the rules need to consider grade level, maturity level, special needs, etc., of students. Is it reasonable to expect kindergarten children to respond to rules in the same way as fifth graders? Normally a kindergartner picking on a fifth grader is considered less critical than a fifth grader picking on a kindergartner.

While classroom rules are the prerogative of the individual classroom teacher and the students in that class, they must conform to, complement and reinforce general school rules. If there is a school rule against chewing gum principals need to feel confident that enforcement of this rule is school-wide.

Rules should be posted in the halls and in the classrooms. Public address announcements and reminders at assemblies are opportunities for principals to reinforce and clarify rules and the consequences for violating them. Students dislike preaching, but they do need to be reminded. Explaining the reasons for rules and their relationship to the real world can help children understand and appreciate reasonable school regulations.

CONSISTENCY OF RULES

Consistency is very important if students are to obey school rules. Students need to know that there is equal justice under the school law. They need to feel that their rights will be protected and infringements on those rights will result in fair, timely, and consistent enforcement of established rules. Exceptions to rules, for any reason, may cause problems for the principal. Every case is different, and individual circumstances of an offense may vary. The principal must make every effort to keep the general school population in mind-but must also remember that some students with special needs and under the protection of regulations such as Pennsylvania's 94-142 (Special Education regulations) may not always be disciplined in the same manner as other students. However, students' disregard for rules and the rights of others should always have consequences. Where suspension is not possible, an in-school timeout or other approaches may be necessary. If withdrawing from transportation privileges is not legally permissible, assigned seats, or other consequence may be permitted.

FIELD TRIPS

Field trips should be approved by the school board. Once approved, these trips are the responsibility of the building principal. Each field trip should provide educational opportunities for student growth beyond the classroom. Travel to an event or site away from school grounds can reinforce and enliven curriculum areas during the school day. While such travel is encouraged, it can become expensive if not regulated. To ensure that the trip is directly related to the curriculum, teachers can present related material before the trip and have students summarize and review topics learned when they return to the classroom. Students need to be reminded that field trips, while out of the ordinary and often seen as more fun than routine school, are important elements of the academic program, and students go on them to broaden their learning experience.

Principals should develop a checklist to monitor all aspects of board-approved trips, similar to the one below.

FIELD TRIP PRE-AUTHORIZATION FORM

Title of Trip _____ Date of Trip _____ Grade Level _____

Trip Facilitator _____ Number of students involved _____

Trip Number _____ Group _____ Board Approved: ☐ Yes ☐ No

Destination and rationale for trip: _____

_____

_____

_____

_____

Transportation:
☐ Bus request submitted   ☐ Request approved

Contingency Plan:
☐ Collection/dispensing of medications   ☐ First aid kits

Itinerary:
☐ Notification of parents   ☐ Permission slips in

Miscellaneous:
☐ Appropriate students involved   ☐ Attendance notified
☐ Specials teacher notified   ☐ Special students included

(This form is to be completed and turned in to the office one week before the date of the trip.)

Using this form, or one like it, will ensure that all vital areas are covered and all safeguards are in place.

WEAPONS AND DRUGS

In recent years, increasing use of weapons in schools has altered many aspects of school life. No longer are comments such as, "I'll kill you," or, " I'll blow your head off," taken as simple joking by school administrators. Such remarks, while usually said in jest or without any real intent to do harm, cause alarm, and principals must address them. Boards of Education have developed policies to address this new area of concern. "Zero tolerance" policies are commonplace, and it is the job of principals, as the first line of defense, to enforce them. However, caution must be exercised when comparing the words and actions of kindergartners with those of high school seniors. Principals and other rule makers must allow for some discretion in application of otherwise black and white regulations. Many would argue that the first grader who brings a small pocketknife to school for show and tell is in a different category from the senior high student who carries a switchblade in his or her jacket pocket. Should the consequences be the same? Should zero tolerance mean automatic expulsion for both students? Does zero tolerance mean that possessing a knife, of any size and by any age student, is not tolerated and consequences will be imposed? Or does it mean automatic expulsion rather than no tolerance? Few school districts tolerate weapons and drugs, but perhaps they do not expel violators automatically.

While knives pose a threat, the possession of a firearm creates a far greater danger. As a result, some schools have taken drastic measures, including installing metal detectors. Most policies state that carrying a gun will result in immediate expulsion and arrest.

Distribution of drugs in school is not a new threat and is common in many schools. Drug-sniffing dogs, locker searches, and strict policies regarding possession of medications are strong indicators that the school is a fertile ground for drug marketing and use. However, with harsh policies, strict, uniform enforcement, and vigilance on the part of administration and staff reduced drug use in schools is possible. Drug use before and after school still remains an area of great concern.

FACILITY MANAGEMENT AND CLIMATE

Managing a modern school building is not an easy job. Principals have to be concerned primarily with use of space to accommodate instruction, but other areas of the facility also require their attention. Storage space must be provided for supplies, equipment, cleaning supplies, and furniture storage. Without such space, schools look messy, and safety and security concerns may arise. Teachers, custodians, secretaries, and food service workers should be involved in deciding how rooms are arranged and used.

Custodians must have secure places to store cleaning supplies. These facilities should be located near the areas that need to be cleaned, should be secure, and, in some cases, be fire resistant because many cleaning fluids are combustible. Additionally, adequate areas must be set aside to store unused furniture, books, audio visual equipment, and other items not used daily.

There must be rooms for staff lunches and conference rooms to meet with parents. Staff lunchrooms allow staff the opportunity to get away from the hustle and bustle of the school day, serve as a place to regroup, and off limits to parents and other nonschool personnel. There is certainly nothing wrong with the principal dropping in for lunch or an informal chat for a few minutes, but the room exists primarily for staff use. Some schools ask student teachers, student aides, and parent volunteers to eat in another area or with the children. All staff are well advised to remember that conversations overheard in the staff lunchroom may be taken out of context by nonprofessionals, and confidentiality may be jeopardized.

To maintain building integrity, inspections are conducted periodically during the school year. Local, state, and federal inspectors may arrive to inspect food service and the kitchen, the general safety of the building, and adherence to employee rights. These inspections should be seen as an opportunity to correct weaknesses in the building before an accident, health concern, or other incident occurs. It is always better to be cited by an inspector and have the opportunity to correct the deficiency than to deal with the consequences of legal action.

The checklist on the following page can serve as a reminder of safety issues to be addressed during the school year.

CHECKLIST FOR SCHOOL SAFETY

Opening of School

□ Check bells (custodial)
□ Check alarm system (custodial)
□ Chain of command (safety)
□ Badge/Sign-in procedure
□ Traffic flow organized
□ "C" team established
□ Phone chain prepared
□ Check playground (custodial)
□ Safety issues in staff, student, parent handbooks
□ Fire drill signs (custodians)
□ Check fire extinguishers (custodians)

□ Phone chain distributed
□ Check weather radio
□ Check door locks (custodial)
□ Communication system setup
□ Emergency inservice to staff
□ Copies of CIP to staff
□ Check building exterior
□ Check sidewalks (custodial)
□ Set up safety committee
□ Set up crisis response team

First Semester

□ Fire drills held - _____-_____-_____-_____-_____-_____
□ Critical incident drill held -_____
□ Building safety committee meetings held - _____-_____-_____
□ Crisis response team meetings - _____-_____-_____-_____
□ Orange "safety" slips submitted as required
□ Review safety concerns with students
□ Tornado drill held - _____
□ Safety inspections conducted - _____-_____-_____-_____

Second Semester

□ Fire drills held - _____-_____-_____-_____-_____-_____
□ Critical incident drill held - _____
□ Building safety committee meetings held - _____-_____-_____
□ Crisis response team meetings - _____-_____-_____-_____
□ Orange "safety" slips submitted as required
□ Tornado drill held - _____
□ Safety inspections conducted - _____-_____-_____-_____

End of the Year

□ Review security efforts for the year
□ Submit summer safety work orders

Aesthetically appealing and orderly buildings are less likely to be vandalized and more likely to motivate students and staff. An attractive environment not only is appealing to visitors but enriches the learning climate throughout the school. Principals should encourage staff, students, and parent groups to help provide the school with colorful, pleasing displays, signs, murals, bulletin boards, and other enhancements to create warm, friendly environments. Schools that care about children often display student works in the hallways and classrooms. Displaying articles of student interest, artwork, certificates, and awards demonstrates the degree of concern for children.

School building safety is more important today than ever before. Inspections of playground equipment, safe hallways and stairwells, secure and safe grounds, and close monitoring of the exterior doors help to keep schools safe.

Quarterly inspections that include the areas listed below can help spot potential problem areas before injuries occur.

Hazard	Date Observed	Correction Needed	Action Taken
Did coworkers handle all wheelchairs in a safe manner?			
Were employees wearing appropriate attire to protect them from wheelchair injury?			
Were any employees observed wearing gloves when washing dishes?			
Were employees observed wearing proper footwear to avoid falls on wet floors?			
Were labels posted on all hot objects indicating a hazard?			
Were custodians observed wearing proper personal protective equipment when cleaning?			
Were custodians moving objects in a safe manner?			
Did custodians appear excessively dirty or dusty?			
Was custodial equipment placed to avoid student and staff injury?			
Were hallways clear of objects that might cause injury in an emergency?			
Were exterior sidewalks clear of objects, snow, ice, etc.?			
Were any materials on the floor that could cause tripping?			

Hazard	Date Observed	Correction Needed	Action Taken
Was anyone seen in an off-balance position standing on chairs, etc.?			
Was anyone seen lifting excessive weight?			
Did professional staff make suggestions for improved safety?			
Were Material Safety Data Sheets available?			
Were all chemicals stored and labeled in approved containers?			
Were science educators wearing protective equipment (glasses)?			
Were science educators observed following good safety procedures?			
Do coworkers know where to locate safety equipment?			
Did any hazards exist in the library that could injure coworkers?			
Did physical education teachers use assistance when moving heavy equipment?			
Were educators observed practicing universal precautions when exposed to body fluids?			
Was proper personal protective equipment readily available?			

Having members of the building safety committee complete such forms helps to monitor safety-related areas. Areas identified as needing attention can then be addressed promptly.

In addition, monitoring potentially violent situations helps to prevent negative consequences. The visibility of the principal and staff throughout the building, good rapport with local police, a positive system to deal with student discipline problems, and support of school board policy are critical parts of any successful protection plan.

CHAPTER 10

THE SCHOOL COMMUNITY

The modern building principal wears many hats.

*The media's relationship with the school can be positive
and supportive, or full of distrust and disharmony.*

Develop PTA support and accept the organization as part of the school.

The principal must communicate proactively.

*Today's schools can be hotbeds of legal controversy interwoven with streaks of
educational brilliance, heavily sprinkled with student achievement.*

PUBLIC RELATIONS

The modern school administrator wears many hats, one of which is school spokesperson. The principal represents the programs, staff, and students in good times and bad, and comments he or she makes can have a tremendously beneficial effect on acceptance of the school's initiatives and, similarly, a devastating effect if they are not well thought out.

One area sometimes overlooked by the busy administrator is the community at large. More and more taxpayers in school districts are nonparents, but they continue to serve as vital supporters of school programs. Principals would be well advised to spread the news about successful programs, achievement on standardized tests, creative and innovative teaching, and other positive school news. Waiting to contact senior citizens and other nonparents until the bond issue is up for a vote or until it's budget time and a new building addition is needed usually results in little, if any, support. Early preparation of the public is critical to the success of any new proposal. One hopes that this communication, with continual nourishment, will grow into support for an improved educational system.

DEALING WITH THE MEDIA

The media relationship with the school system can be positive and supportive or full of distrust and disharmony. Keep in mind that most newspeople are only doing their job, which is reporting the news, both good and bad. While many educators feel that the media look only for sensational, negative stories, the truth is that these stories are reported because people are interested in them. But how does the principal counter the seemingly bad press of failing schools, dropping SAT scores, overpaid teachers, and uncontrollable students?

Most schools have large numbers of parents who work in a wide range of occupations. Staff members have relatives who may have contacts in the news media. In short, a potential source of good news is within each school community. Find out the sources you have as a principal. Research the makeup of your PTA and the relationships its members may have with local media. Cultivate those relationships and become proactive. Call local media and invite them to stop in on a slow news day to discuss your school. Highlight your programs: your excellent staff; your innovative approach to new curricular areas; your successful children in sports, the arts, or academics. Just as the principal must court nonparents in his or her school attendance area, the principal also must seek out and built rapport with the media. Waiting to contact the local television station until after a negative story airs is poor planning. A close working relationship with the media can help to defuse rumors and may help the public develop a better understanding of the educator's role and appreciation of how hard most educators work every day. While being proactive will not stop a negative report, it may soften the story, encourage more in depth investigation before going public, or at least allow the building principal to get the facts out and help present a more balanced coverage.

PTA/PTO

The Parent Teacher Association or Parent Teacher Organization can be a major asset to any school. Parents who want to help make their children's education the best possible experience is key to many programs. Volunteer work, sponsoring special programs and speakers, and providing extra funds in times of tight budgets all contribute to quality in schools. Involve your PTA in the school and make its members feel welcome. Set aside a mailbox for the PTA's use. Support and encourage membership drives and thank the PTA openly and willingly for the help its members give to your school.

Attending PTA functions, and encouraging your staff to attend, shows your support. PTA members are keenly aware of your presence and are more inclined to support your efforts if you endorse their activities. Being at PTA board meetings helps you to address issues before they become major concerns. It allows you to obtain parent support and, in many cases, funding. Most parents and PTA organizations want to support the school. They are major players in their children's education and need to know they are appreciated. Seek their support, gain their trust, and accept them as part of the school team. Principals who disregard the importance of the PTA open the door for increased misinformation, dissatisfaction, and erosion of community support.

NEWSLETTERS

To be successful, the principal must communicate continually with parents and members of the community. The monthly newsletter is an excellent means of expressing the school's position on issues of interest to the school community. Rule enforcement, upcoming events, recognition of student achievements, and areas of community interest should be included. Make the newsletter personal and display your desire for the school to improve an already successful experience. Take the time to write a message worth reading. Parents want to hear what you, as their children's principal, have to say. Be upbeat and positive about the successes and explain areas that need improvement and plans to address them. Most parents may never talk with the principal in person, but most will read the newsletter and thus form a lasting impression of your school and you as the educational leader.

PARENT HANDBOOK

Another valuable means to communicate with parents is the Parent Handbook. Areas to consider for inclusion in the handbook are:

- Principal's message
- Characteristics of the school
- How students are grouped for instruction
- Description of the school board
- Description of central office staff
- Permission slips
- Facts about the district
- Important telephone numbers
- School's mission statement
- Bell schedule
- Lunch schedule
- Attendance policy
- Bus rules
- Special programs (day care, speech, etc.)
- Dress code
- Homework guidelines
- Early dismissal, delayed start, school closings
- Physical education dress code
- Health information
- Security procedures
- Testing procedures and schedule
- Emergency cards
- Parking and student unloading and pickup
- Holiday parties
- Photographing students
- Hints for parents

Such handbooks serve as a reference throughout the school year and help to avoid confusion, misunderstanding, and unnecessary phone calls.

TWO-WAY COMMUNICATION CHANNELS

To be successful, communication must be mutual. Principals must be available to parents and staff and must make every effort to communicate freely with the school internally and the community as a whole. Principals seen as open to the public help to avoid appearing unapproachable or unresponsive. When staff lack access to an uncommunicative principal, a climate of "us vs. them" can result. This mentality can be disastrous to a school's climate.

To open channels of communications, principals often can use local telephone systems that allow voice recording that informs callers of the school's events and other issues of public concern. In technologically equipped districts, e-mail can be a great asset to breaking down information barriers among staff members. Monthly school calendars that outline upcoming events, with updated weekly calendars to allow for changes, can help staff to plan and anticipate needed changes in lessons.

Monthly PTA newsletters are excellent means of communicating with parents. Remember to stress the quality of student academic achievement, staff accomplishments, exciting lessons being presented, upcoming events of interest, and positive aspects of the school. Stressing a school's positive aspects is vital; the news media will take care of the negative events when and if they occur. Make use of monthly PTA meetings to encourage support of programs, highlight staff efforts, and commend overall behavior of the student body.

Many schools use local newspapers to remind the community about upcoming events, and radio and television stations for issues of community interest. If a district has its own public access station, that is an excellent means for showing students at work, quality teaching, and exciting and innovative programs in the schools.

Regardless of the means used, the principal must be proactive in using communication. The days of sitting back and waiting for the media to contact the school for good news are over. Similarly, waiting until a bond issue is being prepared or a tax increase is being considered to "spread the good news" about the school is too little too late. Be honest with the community, admit what areas need attention and the steps that are underway to address them, and plant the seeds of upcoming initiatives long before they are brought into the public eye. If an attendance boundary change is being considered, begin to discuss the problem of too many students in some schools and not enough in others, the size of classes in some buildings, and the challenge the district faces in providing equity across the various schools. Planting seeds that point out the dilemmas the district faces can ease understanding. This preliminary effort can help the community understand why certain actions are needed and may even enlist public support.

SPECIAL EDUCATION

One percent of a school's population can take up 99 percent of the principal's time. Building principals should remember this, especially in regard to special education. Past injustices in the treatment of special education children have resulted in strict laws regulating how these children are to be educated. The building principal must have a good understanding of the Individuals with Disabilities Education Act (IDEA), the federal statute, and the state regulations that govern rights afforded to students who meet eligibility requirements for special education programs. Specifically, IDEA requires that all special education students receive a free and appropriate public education (FAPE). The federal law is the basis for developing State Department of Education regulations that govern how school districts in each state can meet the federal requirements of IDEA.

Adherence to the law is important. School districts that do not meet state and federal requirements are subject to special education due process, state appeals, federal court, circuit court, and supreme court proceedings. This process is very costly in time and money required to defend district positions. It is in the best interest of all for administrative, professional, and paraprofessional staff to be as well versed as possible in IDEA, state regulations, national trends, and best practices in special education.

Principals must know about the following terms and processes:

Child Find

Annual activities conducted in the school to identify students who may be in need of special education services. In addition to formally identified screening activities, such as review of standardized tests and quarterly grade reports, many schools have building-based screening teams that meet weekly to serve this purpose.

Referral

The formal process requesting and receiving a comprehensive evaluation to determine if a child meets eligibility requirements as a student with disabilities who requires specially designed instruction to make meaningful educational progress.

Evaluation

A comprehensive evaluation report (CER) consisting of results compiled by a multidisciplinary team (MDT) that includes the parent, special and regular teacher, and the administrator; a school psychologist usually chairs the team.

Individualized Education Plan (IEP)

A plan developed by the multidisciplinary team when a student has been identified as disabled and requiring specially designed instruction to make meaningful educational progress.

Reevaluation

A comprehensive review of a special education student's continued need for special education programs. In Pennsylvania a reevaluation CER is required at least once every two years for all special education students.

A building principal should be familiar with the following special education terms:

- Notice of Recommended Assignment (NORA)
- Least Restrictive Educational Environment (LRE)
- Local Educational Agency (LEA)
- Family Education Right to Privacy Act (FERPA)
- Emotional Support (ES)
- Learning Support (LS)
- Life Skills Support (LSS)
- Autistic Support (AS)
- Mentally Handicapped (MH)
- Learning Disabled (LD)
- Assistive Technology (AT)
- Physical Therapy (PT)
- Occupational Therapy (OT)

- Speech and Language Pathologist (SLP)
- Student Service Plan (SSP)
- Multidisciplinary Team (MDT)

The special education process begins well before a student is identified as being eligible for special education programs. It starts with a referral that includes documenting what teachers have done to assist the student in the regular education program. For the most part, parents want special help for their children, but prefer that help not be labeled as special education. Every possible alternative should be tried before children are recommended for the comprehensive special education evaluation process. There are building-based screening teams in many schools that help to prepare intervention plans and document strategies that have or have not been successful. After all this has been done is when a student should be referred for possible placement in a special education program.

When a special education evaluation is complete, a student is eligible for special education only when he or she meets eligibility criteria and needs specially designed instruction. The school psychologist usually chairs the multidisciplinary team and assists in writing the comprehensive evaluation report (CER). The MDT makes many recommendations. If a student is disabled but does not need special education classes, the team may recommend that the student have a student service plan (SSP) that outlines reasonable accommodations to the regular school program to assist the student. When and if a student meets both eligibility criteria—that is, a disabling condition that requires specially designed instruction for the student to make meaningful educational progress, and the MDT recommends a special education placement, an IEP is developed, and the student is placed in an appropriate special education program.

A special education student must be educated in the least restrictive educational environment (LRE) with nondisabled peers to the extent possible in the school he or she normally would attend if the student were not disabled. Therefore, school districts must offer a continuum of services consisting of supplemental intervention in the regular classroom and a resource room for students taken out of the regular classroom to acquire basic skills (reading, writing, and math). Most of the time resource rooms and part-time special education classrooms operate in the student's home school. Sometimes more comprehensive services are needed calling for a different curriculum, such as life skills and/or emotional support. This requires a full-time classroom that may be located outside the home school. More restrictive placements outside of the home school or district of a student's residence should be recommended only when the degree of need is such that even with supplemental aides and services, the student has not been successful.

Once a student has been placed in a special education program, the building principal must be very aware of the importance of completing annual IEPs and ensuring that all goals in the IEP are met. The principal plays an important role in developing and monitoring the IEPs.

First, as the IEP is being developed, the principal must be sure that all services and goals included in the IEP can be delivered and met. Second, it is in the best interest of the student, school, and district for all staff to be aware of the rights afforded special education students in regular and special education programs. If the student does not make reasonable progress toward IEP goals, a parent could claim that the student was denied a free and appropriate public education (FAPE). This type of claim can be the subject of a special education due process hearing.

In Pennsylvania, for example, when a parent makes a claim that his or her special education child has been denied FAPE, the parent has a right to an impartial due process hearing before a state due process hearing officer. This process is afforded to parents of students with disabilities by state regulations and defined in the federal law (IDEA).

Entering into a due process hearing demands a great deal of professional time and taxpayers' money. Special education due process is a legal proceeding whereby the school district and the parents each are represented by an attorney. Legal documents are prepared, and witnesses present direct testimony and are subject to cross examination on the witness stand. Each attorney tries to discredit the opposing side's witnesses. This process results in a very expensive, emotional, and draining experience for all. Within thirty days of the end of the hearing, the state hearing officer writes an opinion determining the disposition of the issue. If either party disagrees with the hearing officer's opinion, an appeal can be made in Pennsylvania to a state three-attorney appeal panel. If a party disagrees with the appellate decision, the appeal panel's decision can be appealed to the appropriate district court. The district court decision can then be appealed to the appropriate circuit court.

If and when a decision is finally made, if the parents prevail, a district has to pay the parents' attorney fees, per the parent's attorney fees provision of IDEA. As you can see, a wise principal will not allow special education issues to get out of control in his or her building.

In addition to the educational program, discipline issues can create concerns in special education. When discipline problems arise among special education students, the administrator must understand the legal implications before taking action. There are protections afforded special education students that are not afforded regular students. When a special education student is excluded from school, or from a related service such as transportation, for more than fifteen cumulative days in a given school year, it is considered a significant change in educational placement. A significant change in placement cannot be implemented without first convening the MDT. For example, a non-special education student may be suspended from school for an unlimited number of days during the school year. A special education student may only be suspended only for a cumulative fifteen days during any school year, with no one exclusion to exceed ten days. If a special education student violates the school discipline policy, and consequences require more than the permitted fifteen days in a school year, the MDT must meet to determine if the behavior was a manifestation of the student's disability. This determination is documented in a comprehensive reevaluation report and presented to the parents. If the behavior is not related to the student's disability, the special education student may be excluded from school for more than fifteen cumulative days, providing his or her parents agree to the exclusion. A NORA is presented to the parents, who are given the opportunity to disapprove. If the parent disapproves, the district must proceed to an impartial special education due process hearing to go forth with the disciplinary exclusion. It is very important that principals understand the ramifications of improperly excluding special education students because of disciplinary infractions. Often before a disciplinary exclusion is recommended, the MDT meets to resolve the issue differently.

Regular teachers must be educated about the process and procedure for teaching students with disabilities in the regular classroom. Teachers must be aware of state-of-the-art practices in dealing with regular and special education student needs in the classroom. The administrator must make techniques available to staff that address special needs. The concepts of adaptive curriculum and grading, co-teaching with a special education teacher, and adjusted workload for some children must be accepted. Specifically, teachers need help to understand the seriousness of providing appropriate accommodations and adaptations for students in regular classes. This applies not only to students with IEPs but also to those who may be identified as disabled but do not require special education classes. A disabled student who does not have an IEP does have a student service plan (SSP), which outlines an educational plan for him or her. Teachers have to know that they may be expected to make written adaptations and accommodations for identified students. A few years ago, newspapers headlines read, "Inclusion: It's a right, not a privilege," which has become the subject of numerous special education due process hearings.

Relationships with the parent or guardian are important if parents and teachers are to work together. The administrator must learn to work with all kinds of personalities and remember that parents and others involved in the process have the best interest of the child at heart. The ability to work with others is a vital part of any administrator's position, and is especially important with parents of special education children.

In most school districts, the building principal does not make decisions about special education processes, programs, and situations alone. Special education supervisors should be able to provide resources needed in the buildings to ensure that special education services are available. They can provide leadership in best practices, national trends, legal requirements, and funding needs, and ensure that the district is operating sound, compliant programs. A special education supervisor can be a great advocate for special education programs and students within the school.

The building principal is the first person to meet with parents, regular education teachers, and special education teachers throughout the year. He or she must establish an environment within the school that shows a concern for all children. Proactive actions that support a strong belief in the rights of all children set the tone of acceptance and cooperation within the building. Knowing, learning, and understanding special education requirements; treating all concerned with respect; and expecting high levels of professional commitment are well worth the time investment. This approach is a vast improvement over that of reacting to a situation that could have been avoided had the principal been knowledgeable about school district responsibilities and special education parents' and students' due process rights.

SCHOOL LAW

More and more, the school is becoming a legal-, regulatory-, rights-oriented institution as well as an educational one. Many may not like this, but that is the way it is, and the future holds no promise of reversing this trend. As schools begin to support, enhance, or assume the responsibilities of society (teenage driving, drinking, pregnancy, drugs, building self-esteem, protecting student rights, security from violence, etc.), school principals spend more time dealing with legal issues. Protecting the rights of specific students, while making sure that such rights do not interfere with the rights of others (inclusion of an emotionally handicapped child in a regular class), can add frustration and stress to the principal's life. Dealing with parents who feel their complaint or grievance warrants legal help may consume tremendous amounts of the principal's time and effort. Addressing mixed custody, single-parent and divorced spouse, adherence to residency requirements, and enforcement of attendance laws all add to the principal's legal obligations. A lack of attention to legal details can result in action being taken against the district, the school board, and/or the individual building principal. Truly, today's principal must wear many hats to be a successful educational leader and survive in the modern educational world.

LEGAL ASPECTS IN RELATION TO PUBLIC SCHOOL STUDENTS

Only three groups of individuals are required to inhabit places that they do not wish to. These groups are prisoners, mental patients, and public school students. Because of this, courts are very concerned about their treatment. And, in many cases, the courts are most concerned about students and protecting their rights.

School districts lose large numbers of court cases because they lack common sense. Review of some court decisions causes the rational principal to ask, "Why would a district do such a stupid thing?" Federal courts have held that schools must:

- Educate *all* students.
  That means special education, discipline problems, emotional problems, children of difficult parents, every heritage, and every religion.
- Provide a safe and orderly environment for *all* students.
  Make every effort to create a secure climate for learning to take place, free from distractions that interfere with the educational process.
- Provide for the health, safety, and welfare for *all* students.
  Create a positive environment where student conflict is dealt with in a positive, proactive manner.

At the same time, principals must avoid actions that are perceived as:

- arbitrary-selected at random and without reason;
- capricious-apt to change suddenly or unpredictably; or
- deliberately indifferent—to ponder issues without taking action.

To guard against charges of being arbitrary, principals should make certain that they:

- are well informed about the particulars of each case;
- investigate both sides of a manner thoroughly;
- reach a logical conclusion based on the known facts; and
- take appropriate action to deal with the situation and avoid a recurrence of the incident.

In investigating school-related student problems, school officials have an advantage over law enforcement officials. In relation to issues having to do with search and seizure law enforcement officials must have reasonable cause, while principals need only demonstrate reasonableness. This advantage is easier to understand when we realize that reasonable cause requires a 97.5 percent assurance of illegality, while reasonableness needs only 51 percent assurance that wrongdoing has taken place.

Staff legal issues can cause difficult problems. When a situation arises in a school that involves a staff member, the principal must not attempt to avoid embarrassment or lower morale. Two different approaches to dealing with staff-related cases are principal directed and central office directed. In the principal-directed example, the principal is the key investigator. He or she must serve as the unbiased interviewer, listening willingly to allegations, document testimony, and report findings to the central office. This approach can cause strong reactions in the principal's building. There have been cases where investigation of staff members accused of misconduct has been divisive. In such cases, the principal may be viewed as "out to get" the staff member or nonsupportive of his or her staff.

The second approach is an investigation instigated by central office personnel. In this approach, individuals or a team from the central office investigate, interview, collect data, and recommend consequences regarding the staff member in question. This avoids placing the principal in an untenable position, and allows the school to continue operating in a fairly normal manner without the feeling that the principal is lurking around looking for information. When and if a decision is made to suspend or terminate an employee, it results in less damage to the principal's position.

Regardless of the approach used, the principal must regain staff confidence, attempt to keep emotions out of the school, and maintain the learning environment-no easy task!

Principals must learn how to deal with students' rights so that individual rights are protected while they maintain a safe and well-run school. Be conscientious of due process procedures and make certain that you ask the right questions in the right manner. Be fully aware of special education mainstreaming regulations and the special procedures you must follow in disciplining specific students. Be careful of scheduling classes, offering programs, student-to-student interchanges, and staff-to-student communications to avoid issues of discrimination (sexual or otherwise). Review safety issues with your staff often to help offset concerns about injuries and liabilities that may result. Remind staff (especially secretaries) of the need for confidentiality in all aspects of school life. What happens in school, stays in school and even then it is discussed only with those who need to know. Meet regularly with student aides, student teachers and parent volunteers in the school to review confidentiality matters. Anyone who is a part of your school must abide by rules created to protect everyone.

INFORMAL AND FORMAL BOARD MEETINGS TO CONSIDER POLICY VIOLATIONS

While individual districts may have specific procedures for student disciplinary hearings, they must provide basic due process protection. Students have rights guaranteed by both state and federal laws.

When students are accused of a serious violation of a school policy or rule, many districts require:

- Parent notification by certified mail to provide proof of such notification.
- Informing the parents about
  — what the student is accused of doing,
  — what rule or policy the student is alleged to have violated,
  — what rights the student is entitled to, and
  — when the informal hearing has been scheduled
- At an informal hearing, at which place: the information cited above is reviewed.
  — Notes are taken of discussions that take place, including the students response and others' testimony. (If student witnesses are used, they must be available for cross examination.)
- After the informal hearing, a certified letter be sent to parents, which includes:
  — a restatement of the date of informal hearing;
  — the date and time of the scheduled formal hearing;
  — all due process rights afforded to the student; and
  — a list of witnesses who may be called.

There are two types of formal hearings before the school board: the due process or evidence phase, and penalty phase.

- Included in the due process/evidence phase:
  — a statement that all due process requirements have been met: student received proper notice and student understood the policy
  — the specific policy alleged to have been violated; and
  — testimony of the principal about data collected relating to the specific violation.

After the board renders its decision, and if the student did in fact violate the specific policy or rule, the penalty phase begins. It includes:

  — the principal's recommendation of a penalty or consequence for the violation;
  — the reasons for such recommendation; and
  — the principal's accounting of extenuating circumstances, attendance records, disciplinary record, grades, etc.

The Board then determines the appropriate consequence for the violation and votes to suspend or expel the student at a public meeting.

What will be the effect of suspending a student found in possession of a drug or a weapon; or smoking? How will the parents respond to the letter sent from the principal about the referral to the magistrate for truancy? When will the parents' attorney call regarding the suspension from school pending a hearing before the school board for possible expulsion? How will the union deal with the grievance in reference to the extra duty you assigned the math teacher? When and how will the special education advocate meet to discuss the ground rules needed before scheduling the mediation session with the state mediator? Today's schools can be hotbeds of legal controversy interwoven with streaks of educational brilliance, heavily sprinkled with student achievement.

NEGOTIATIONS AND THE BUILDING PRINCIPAL

The building principal often is not involved formally in contact talks with negotiating groups. This is wise because the principal has to maintain a good rapport with staff, and sitting on the other side of the negotiations table can cause disagreements and hard feelings. Principals usually should serve as backup and perhaps as part of the caucus group. At the very least, every building principal should make notes during the duration of the current contract about problems in enforcement, language interpretation, and timeliness of implementation, and communicate any concerns to the district negotiations team. Principals need to remember that the district team does not have to implement the issues agreed to in the contract; the principals do. So, it is in their best interest to have input into the contract that they have to abide by for the next few years.

Contract enforcement is a very important matter. On review of the new contract with staff, remind them that *it is the principal's job* to enforce the agreed-upon contract. And just as they should (and will) hold you accountable for living up to your end of the agreement, they also are required to follow contractual matters. That means a teacher being late to work, a custodian taking an extended lunch, or a secretary sharing private matters with others has to be addressed. Disregarding one incident, an unexcused lateness, one extra-long lunch, or one indiscreet comment sends the message that the behavior is acceptable. Moreover, you are opening the door to accusations of unfairness or arbitrariness when you do try to enforce a similar infraction that you have overlooked previously. For your own peace of mind, make no exception that you cannot justify, show no favoritism that you cannot afford, and take no action that you cannot defend.

ADMINISTERING CONTRACTS

The building principal is responsible for knowing the teachers' contract inside and out. This legal agreement between the school district and the teachers can be either a tool for effective operation or a continual area of disagreement and hostility. Most teachers recognize that the building principal has a job to do. They accept this as long as the principal is reasonable, fair, and consistent in applying rules and responding to requests. The teachers' contract may outline the steps required for assigning staff, time periods for notice regarding classroom observations, the right, as administrator, to place students in classes, and the process to be used in the event of a disagreement between teacher and principal. Scheduling the correct number of teaching classes permitted as outlined in the contract, can avoid a grievance. Transferring a teacher to another grade level without checking the contract may prove upsetting and embarrassing when the teacher must be moved back. The principal's knowledge of the contract is crucial to avoiding problems that can consume an enormous amount of time. This can be avoided if proper procedure is followed.

It is wise to have at least two copies of the contract, one in the office and one at home. A late night call about the death of an uncle and the allowed amount of leave can be answered quickly and accurately.

It should be noted that whatever the group involved, a contract works both ways. It is a safeguard for the teacher, custodian, or secretary, but it also includes regulations he or she must follow. Starting and ending times, length of lunch period, responsibilities of the position, reports to be completed, and evaluation procedures normally are included and are legal agreements between staff members and the district. Just remember to use, not abuse, the contract.

CHAPTER 11

THE FUTURE

*Forces outside the school can have a major
impact on change within the system.*

*To be effective, principals must be responsive to the public they serve and reflect that
public's values and interests throughout the school.*

*Staff, parents, and the community must work
together to develop long-range goals.*

Every district should have a vision, a focus, and reason for existence.

*Educators cannot be all things to all people,
and schools cannot cure all of society's ills.*

There are no shortcuts and no book has all the right answers.

SCHOOLS AND COMMUNITY VALUES AND INTERESTS

Successful public school systems reflect the social values and interests of the communities they serve. These values should be the basis of curriculum innovation, policy implementation, and programs in individual schools. In many communities, special interest groups become very influential, reminding the school of its responsibility to incorporate community values into the system.

Principals must remember that forces outside the school can have a major impact on change within the system, and efforts to listen and respond to such forces can mean the difference between the success or failure of programs. The very name *public schools* suggests that the public's values should be the ultimate controlling factor regarding what is taught, how it is taught, and how schools operate. Local taxpayers may demonstrate concern about course offerings, staff selection, staff retention, or dismissal of staff. Additionally, through court action, issues related to students rights, special education, or suspension of students, the community may influence educational change. The alternative is political action through local elections or pressure on the individual school.

Many schools try to reflect the society in which they operate and provide the best educational system possible. This approach sometimes is motivated by administrative initiatives or an alteration in process adaption. It also can be an activity initiated to reshape existing programs in response to political pressure. Clearly, some pressure groups are more vocal and, occasionally, more successful in influencing program implementation.

Although the public ultimately has the option of replacing elected school board members and applying pressure to replace ineffective administrators, communities frequently find basic values and interests reflected in school programs. When they are not reflected, it is not a deliberate refusal to do so by school officials, but a result of the difficulty in determining the true feelings of a large, diverse population. To be effective, principals must be responsive to the public they serve and reflect that public's values and interests throughout the school.

PLANNING AND COPING WITH CHANGE

Educational change sometimes fails partly because of principal's assumptions and partly because some problems may be inherently unsolvable.

In the past, principals often were not sensitive to the need for a theory of change. Effective educational planners have to combine their expertise in and knowledge of the direction or nature of change with an understanding of, and an ability to deal with, existing factors. Sometimes it is not the change that is objected to, but the process used to implement the change.

Principals need to undertake a critical assessment of a proposed change and consider whether the change is truly in line with school goals. They also need to consider whether implementing the change is truly possible. Some problems are so complex, they cannot be amenable to solution because of too many variables and an inability to get others to act on them. In addition, principals need to consider the availability of needed technical expertise and the interpersonal and technical skills required to implement the change.

The most fundamental problem is that principals and other planners of change often do not have adequate formal training or on-the-job preparation to be change leaders. Principals who want to effect change need to determine the need to move in a particular direction, and to what extent existing factors are conducive or resistant to implementing change. Involvement of staff is critical in any change. Whether the district or school community can be influenced to support change depends on the existence of favorable conditions. The most successful examples of change have occurred when current leaders are replaced with new ones with different characteristics who respond to a mandate for change.

LONG-RANGE PLANS

Principals must look continually for ways to improve their schools. While long-range plans often are formulated at the central office level, the principal must ask where he or she wants the school to be in two, five, and ten years? Should the principal reorganize teaching teams, restructure the classroom arrangement, develop a peer mediation program, departmentalize grades, or plan for facility improvement?

Steps to consider when developing a proposed strategic plan include:

1. Scan the internal and external environment.
2. Outline the organizational structure and transitional outcome.

3. Investigate personnel, facilities, library and other resources.
4. Develop vision, belief, and mission statements.
5. Set goals.
6. Develop student learning and transition outcomes.
7. Set graduation requirements.
8. Set priorities for action plans.
9. Develop action plans for planned courses of study at the elementary and secondary levels.
10. Develop an assessment plan.
11. Develop an induction and professional development plan.

When related to the school's mission, these long-range plans help to motivate staff and insure the likelihood that the change will take place. The principal must formulate long-range goals in concert with staff, parents, and the community. Intermediate steps must be in place to serve as gauges of successful movement. These short-term objectives also provide an opportunity to make needed corrections. They allow evaluation of the procedures, processes, and stages of development before costly mistakes are made.

Once formed, these long-term goals should be advertised to the public. This provides several benefits. One, it announces publicly the goal and helps to gain public support. Two, it makes it more difficult for the school to rescind action toward its goals. Three, it serves as a target of or focus for action. Remember, only aim for attainable goals that now are just beyond reach, but with planning and effort are within the realm of possibility.

VISION STATEMENTS

Every district should have a vision. A vision is a direction, a focus, a reason for existence. It is a goal toward which all district activities are directed. These statements should be the combined product of the entire school community, including the teaching staff, support groups, administrators, parents, and students. Involving all aspects of the district is key to enhancing feelings of ownership. A sample statement follows:

> The Summerset School District is dedicated to providing a quality education to the children of the district to open the doors to the future through academic achievement, computer literacy, and a successful life as a contributing member of society.

After the district "vision statement" is developed, a mission statement is written that describes in more detail how the vision will be accomplished. It addresses the direction and course to follow and states priorities and the commitment to a given course. Mission statements should meet the following criteria:

• Tell why the school exists and what makes it unique.
• Be designed for *one* district or one school.
• Be short and easy to remember.
• Suggest certain goals and give a screen through which to evaluate the appropriateness of any given goal.

These broad steps provide the direction for schools to follow. A sample mission statement might be:

> The Summerset School District is dedicated to providing each individual student the fullest opportunity to reach his or her individual potential through a concentrated, relevant curriculum taught by professional educators. It is the mission of our district to meet every student's needs, motivate and enhance self-confidence, and prepare every child to be an active, contributing member of our society.

Following the mission statement, individual schools should prepare their own mission statement to describe and delineate their role further in reaching the district's mission and, ultimately, the vision of the school community. The principal leads the way with the help of staff and community involvement. The committee should look at where the school *is* and where it *should be* in the future. A worthy school mission statement is meant to *close the gap*. It communicates the school's goal to the community and gives purpose to the schools' daily activities.

To help in developing the individual school's mission, the principal should be sure that the statement:

- is articulated clearly (symbolic actions, time allocations);
- is in place before school improvement efforts begin;
- represents all stakeholders: community, special education, nonparents;
- has the commitment of the committee members;
- looks at philosophy of education, child growth and development, role of teachers and parents in the process;
- is written in short, logically connected statements that clearly reflect specific goals, is no more than a page in length, serves as a guide for future orientations, and symbolizes the community's commitment;

Finally, any changes made in the school should be done so with the mission statement in mind.

A school mission statement might read as follows:

> Grandview School is dedicated to providing an excellent foundation of quality education through team teaching by concerned, professional teams of teachers within a positive, enriching environment. Here every child is special, and opportunity is available for every child to develop to his or her fullest potential. In cooperation with parents and the community, the staff promotes self-esteem, good citizenship, self-discipline, and the love of learning.

The mission statement of the school might be illustrated as in the sample on the following page.

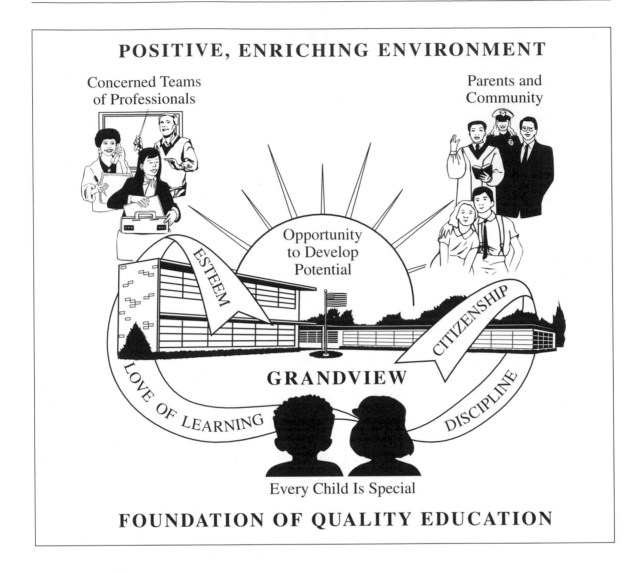

The individual school's mission should reinforce the district's initiatives while being more specific on how they will be accomplished. The next step is for schools to set specific goals to address their mission statement. These goals are usually one year in duration and include a specific timeline for completion.

Every activity, every action, and every event within an individual school should be related to the school's mission, which in turn, is related to the district mission and, ultimately, the vision of the school district.

LEADERSHIP IN THE FUTURE

If education is to serve as the basis for developing the potential of young people and empower them to shape their world of the future, it is vital that principals realize the influence they have. Next to the students and teachers, the principals are the most important element in education. They are responsible for monitoring and improving the teaching of the young, not only to prepare for the future, but also to adapt to changes in their world. Although important, the cafeteria, library, transportation, central office, and other support personnel are only ancillary. Schools do not exist to produce an outstanding library, although a well-stocked library is a great asset. Schools do not exist to serve thousands of nutritious meals, although a healthy body is critical to the successful learner. Schools do not occupy their positions to develop student hotels, although clean, well-run housing is important to student welfare. Participants in education must assess their importance in the overall development of the child. Everyone involved must remember that the the primary reason they are in their present position is for the education of youth. Any young adult who leaves our school system without the necessary tools for life serves as an indictment of every educator. Everyone, from the custodian to the superintendent of schools, exists for one purpose: to educate children.

District priorities must reflect the central goal of quality education. A vision must be developed that reflects the direction of the district and forms the core of all of the parts of the educational program. The first and most important mission must be supporting the teacher in the classroom. Teachers must be serviced by principals, principals serviced by the central office and the superintendent, and the superintendent supported by the board of education. It is time to get the school's priorities in order once again. Educators cannot be all things to all people. Our schools cannot cure all of society's ills.

The recent addition of areas better handled by the family and/or by other agencies, such as health agencies, or by the police departments, juvenile probation system, and social workers, only dilutes the effectiveness of the schools in performing their primary role of teaching children to read, write, and develop their thinking skills. This question remains: If schools no longer accept responsibility for such diverse areas, will these agencies once again become more viable institutions?

When looking at schools, we need to examine the current offerings to students. How broad must the offerings be to provide a proper and useful education that meets the goal of the school's mission? Can the child be prepared for life with an emphasis on basic English and math, or are additional options really necessary?

Principals must begin to monitor classes more closely. Teachers must be held accountable for the progress of their students. Real thought must be given to techniques used in teaching. The lecture-so often found in the public school setting-must be suspect, and more emphasis should be given to quality questions, relevant homework that truly challenges children, and evaluations of both students and teachers that measure comprehension and success.

Leaders in the education field, including principals, superintendents, and supervisors, must begin to take a firm stand in support of clear missions for educational institutions. They must begin to say no when confronted by requests for the addition of curriculum areas that do not relate to their vision for education in America. Schools should be involved only in areas that have a direct effect on children's ability to learn. This will not be easy. Historically, educators have said, "Yes, we will try to help the child adjust to society, overcome his destructive tendencies, relate in an acceptable sexual manner, and understand his parents' inequities." To alter that stance and become resistant undoubtedly will be viewed as rebellion and uncooperative by the general public.

The idea of principals being agents of change is not new. However, the thought that principals, as well as other educational leaders, can and should take firm hold of the direction education is going and dictate its course may be revolutionary to many. If change is to take place in tomorrow's schools, however, and if education is to rise above the mediocrity so prevalent today, principals must develop missions that set a vision for their schools. If public schools are to compete with private schools, charter schools, and other educational reform movements, they must be proactive. Public schools must publicize their strengths, highlight their successes, and continually seek to improve their weaknesses. School missions cannot solve all of society's problems, but as viable institutions devoted to developing children's minds, they must strive to prepare today's youth to become active participants in a changing world.

SUMMARY

School administrators fulfill many roles within the public eye today. Every school principal must approach each day with a well-developed plan and be prepared for a variety of events, some beyond his or her control. These events, ranging from the mundane to dramatic, alter prepared plans, interfere with well-developed timelines, and test the principal's fortitude and ability. While principals can never be fully prepared for every occurrence, they must have skills and knowledge adequate to meet the challenges. Failure to be proactive, or responding to situations without knowledge and common sense, contributes to disharmony within the staff, mistrust from parents, and an unsafe school climate.

The issues discussed here only partially address the many tasks and challenges faced by today's principal. New and interesting events arrive at the office door every day. Many of these events call on the principal to be creative, reactive, and logical. There are no shortcuts, no books full of all the answers, and no matrices to cover all of the decisions needed each day.

It is hoped that through the shared ideas and experiences of the author, the journey through the principalship may be less hazardous, result in less frustration, and, in the end, be more fulfilling and rewarding for the "keeper of the dream," the elementary building principal.

About the Author

Dr. Larry J. Stevens received his bachelor's degree from Pennsylvania State University, two master's degrees from Edinboro University of Pennsylvania, and an Ed.D. in school administration from the University of Buffalo. In addition to teaching in public schools for thirteen years, he earned a Superintendent's Letter of Eligibility, Certification as Supervisor of Curriculum and Instruction, and Administrative Certification in both elementary and secondary administration. Dr. Stevens has served as a secondary and elementary building principal for the past twenty-one years and has taught graduate classes in school administration at Edinboro University of Pennsylvania.

His previous publications include:

Administrative Planning Guide, Edinboro, L. J. Stevens Educational Publications, 1985.

"Administrative Techniques—The Principal's Time," *NASSP Bulletin* 68 (468), January 1984: 59–63.

"Instructional Leadership: A Single District Study of the Multiple Perceptions of Central Office Administrators, Principals, and Elementary Principals," University of New York at Buffalo, April 1996.

"Development of a Critical Incident Plan," Principals' Profile, PAESSP, December 1997.

"Development of a Critical Incident Plan," ADMINISTRATOR, PAESSP, February, 2000.